W9-CIF-913

"Lately it occurs to me, what a long, strange trip it's been . . ."

"Truckin'"—The Grateful Dead
(Robert Hunter, Jerry Garcia, Phil Lesh, Bob Weir)

The Steam Locomotive

A CENTURY OF NORTH AMERICAN CLASSICS

JIM BOYD

MetroBooks

DEDICATION

To Doyle McCormack and Jack Wheelihan of the
Southern Pacific Daylight 4449 crew, who always made
me feel welcome around their "toys"

PHOTOGRAPHY

Color photography by Jim Boyd except as indicated

Copyright © 2000 by Andover Junction Publications
This edition published by MetroBooks by arrangement
with Andover Junction Publications.

2002 MetroBooks

ISBN 1-5866-3613-8

Printed and bound in China
02 03 04 05 06 07 MC 11 10 9 8 7 6 5 4 3 2

For bulk purchases and special sales, please contact:
Friedman/Fairfax Publishers
Attention: Sales Department
230 Fifth Avenue, Suite 700-701
New York, NY 10001
212/685-6610 Fax 212/685-3916

LFA

Edited by Mike Schafer and Maureene D. Gulbrandsen. Book design and layout by Mike Schafer, Andover Junction Publications, Lee, Illinois, and
Blairstown, New Jersey. Technical assistance by Jim Popson.

ACKNOWLEDGEMENTS: The author would like to thank all those who contributed data and imagery, either knowingly or otherwise, to this project.
Many of the black & white images were borrowed from the extensive photo
archives of *Railfan & Railroad* Magazine, published by Carstens Publications (P. O. Box 700, Newton, NJ 07860), while others were contributed
directly to the author over the years from people like Jim Shaughnessy, J. J.
Young Jr., Homer R. Hill, Robert F. Collins, John Krause, and Charles Felstead.
Color images were contributed by Mike Del Vecchio, Mike Schafer, Russ
Porter, Ken Ganz, Steve Brown, and Patrick Golden. The authors of the hundreds of books that were used to research this project are far too numerous
to list individually, but their efforts have contributed immeasurably to the
preservation and dissemination of railroad and locomotive history.

A special thanks must go to my longtime friend Mike Schafer who
designed and laid out this book, and to Steve Esposito of Andover Junction
Publications, the producers of this book for Barnes & Noble, who made the
entire project possible.

A final special thanks goes out to all of you throttle-jockey "stars" and
nameless grease-covered "grunts" who keep them on the spectacular stage
of mainline steam operations. You are the ones who truly made this book a
reality with your long hours, hard work, and selfless dedication.

FRONT COVER: One of the most famous American steam locomotives of all
time, a Pennsylvania Railroad Class K4s Pacific, returned to life on April 12,
1987, in the same Juniata Shop complex in Altoona, Pennsylvania, where it
had been built in May 1918. The 1361, which had been on display at Horseshoe Curve for 28 years, was restored by Doyle McCormack's crew for the
Railroaders Memorial Museum of Altoona and operated a number of excursion trips in the area. On this first night of renewed life, the 1361 was being
test run within the Juniata Shop complex and was posed for this nocturnal
portrait by the author.

FRONTISPIECE: Grand Trunk Western 2-8-2 No. 4070 was rolling out a
majestic plume of smoke as it accelerated eastward near Stillwell, Indiana,
on a GTW excursion from Chicago to South Bend in November 1968.

TITLE PAGE: In an ultimate expression of the possibilities of preserved
and restored steam, on August 8, 1991, two Van Sweringen Berkshires,
Pere Marquette 1225 and Nickel Plate 765, were posed for a night photo
session in the CSX 20th Street Yard in Huntington, West Virginia, during
the National Railway Historical Society national convention. The stormy
night created an amazing atmosphere of a working railroad yard of the
late 1940s.

Contents

(Above left) A steam locomotive thrives on the elements of fire and water—and it's even maintained by fire. As with automobiles, steam locomotives have tires, but when they require changing it takes more than a jack and tire iron to do the job. To place it over the wheel center casting, the steel tire has to be expanded by heat and carefully aligned. When it cools the tire will grip the wheel tighter than any bolt could hold it. This timeless procedure is being performed in 1988 at the Steamtown National Historic Site in Scranton, Pennsylvania. *(Ken Ganz)*

(Left) Reading 4-8-4 2102 is steaming away the night at Raritan, New Jersey, in February 1972 between excursion trips for the High Iron Company on the Jersey Central.

Introduction

The Chesapeake & Ohio main line from Huntington to Hinton, West Virginia, has changed little since the C&O was running its own 2-8-4s there. In October 1988 the Fort Wayne Railroad Historical Society's Nickel Plate 2-8-4 765 was departing Charleston on a "New River Train" excursion over CSX to Hinton and back.

The familiar image of Gauley Bridge, West Virginia, can be seen over the shoulder of fireman Tom Stephens as the Lima-built 2-8-4 marches eastward on the double-track main line of the Chesapeake & Ohio. For the past hour we've been working eastward along the south bank of the Kanawha River with a 30-car passenger train, maintaining the track speed of 40 MPH. From here east to Hinton, however, the C&O traverses the spectacular New River Gorge.

We're climbing a .38 percent grade, which is giving the locomotive a good workout. But from here to Cotton Hill, about six miles ahead, the grade increases to .48 percent (a rise of 4.8 feet every 1,000 feet). This is the toughest part of the run. Fireman Stephens has his stoker set at a comfortable rate, feeding bituminous coal into the inferno of the firebox. The feedwater pump is keeping the boiler constantly resupplied with water. Engineer Rich Melvin has his hands full on this October day, for the weather has been

wet, and the colorful autumn leaves that fall onto the rails and get mashed beneath the wheels are an effective lubricant, making the track a little slipperier than usual.

The sound of the exhaust is reverberated back from the rocky cliffs on the south side of the train. Adding a stereo-effect counterpoint is the same sound echoing back off the other side of the valley, its distance-induced delay enhancing the chaos. The stoker is rumbling underfoot, and you can detect the rushing sound of the water pump. Inside the cab, your whole world is overwhelmed with sound and motion, laced with the not unpleasant aroma of soft coal smoke, hot oil, and cool autumn air.

It is an aberration in the sound that propels engineer Melvin into quick action. The driving wheels have broken loose into a furious uncontrollable spin. He slams the throttle shut and snaps it right back out again, trying to stop the slip without losing speed and momentum. The wheels catch hold, and the exhaust steadies . . . only to break loose again. Once more the throttle is violently closed and swiftly reopened. The first sign of a wheel slip on an engine working this hard is a subtle shudder through the frame that can usually be caught with a quick application of the sand valve before a full slip develops. When she shudders here, though, the sand doesn't scotch it, and Rich has to work the throttle.

The footing is solid once more, but we've lost two miles per hour and are now down to 32. Rich drops the reverse lever forward a notch to give the cylinders a bigger bite of steam. Fireman Stephens has the steam pressure right on the peg at 245 psi (pounds per square inch). The engine is so hot that every time Rich closes the throttle, the first safety valve pops when he reduces his use of the steam.

The cylinder pressure gauge beside the throttle is a good measure of how hard the engine is working. Accelerating on level track it had been as high as 210 psi, but on the slippery rail of the hill, anything above 140 will cause her to slip. Rich figures he needs 150 psi to hold a steady speed on this climb and 175 psi to accelerate. When she slips at 140, you start losing ground to the hill.

The sound is awesome as we swing past the Cotton Hill depot and crest the grade. The speed is about 19 MPH, but the battle is won. By the time the 30th passenger car clears the depot, it's gliding along at about 30 MPH under a gentle "rain" of cinders from the laboring locomotive. Once again Rich and his crew will "put 'er into Hinton on time."

This drama, once so common in America, did not take place in 1948 or even 1958. It was on October 16, 1988. Locomotive 765 was built in 1944 for the Nickel Plate Road and overhauled in the late 1970s by the Fort Wayne Railroad Historical Society in Indiana. In "real life," Rich Melvin runs a videotape production company, and fireman Tom Stephens owns a lumber mill in Ohio. The train was made up of privately owned passenger cars, and the trip was sponsored by the Huntington (West Virginia) Chapter of the National Railway Historical Society. CSX Transportation, the corporate successor to the Chesapeake & Ohio, was one of the many large railroads at that time that would work with private steam locomotive operators.

For all practical purposes, the steam era ended in the U.S. in 1960. Only one major railroad, the Union Pacific, has operated its own excursion locomotives continuously since the end of steam; its last new steam locomotive, 4-8-4 No. 844, has never been off the active roster since it was built in December 1944. All other mainline steam locomotives operating in America have been resurrected after retirement.

It is interesting to note today that since 1960, examples of nearly every significant type of American steam locomotive have been brought back to life by museums, tourist opera-

tors, historical groups, or mainline railroads. Although the trains they haul and the railroads over which they run can vary from totally authentic to completely ridiculous, the

locomotives themselves are quite genuine—and when running under steam they are as "authentic" as they ever were, particularly on those occasions when they can perform near their design limits. Even though the mixed-bag train of streamlined cars that 765 hauled out of Huntington was unlike anything it had ever seen on the Fort Wayne Division of the Nickel Plate, the weight of that train on Cotton Hill had the locomotive performing right up to the specs that Lima had built into her back in the closing days of World War II.

In this book we will survey the history and development of the American mainline steam locomotive and illustrate it with those that have survived. Not all of the locomotives shown are running today, for even preserved locomotives have practical working life spans that depend on the financial resources of the operating group and the political environment of each situation. The 765 is today undergoing overhaul in Fort Wayne, and

CSX is reluctant to operate steam, but meanwhile entirely different locomotives are operating on railroads that would have seemed politically impossible in 1988.

Since the end of steam we have seen in operation everything from the world's oldest surviving locomotive to two of the largest articulateds ever built and examples of just about every technological step in between. As you go through these pages, the color photos are of locomotives that have operated since 1958, while the black & white photos illustrate engines before their retirement. The color images, all taken since the "end of steam," clearly show that we have done an excellent job of preserving the rich heritage of America's steam locomotives.

Jim Boyd
Crandon Lakes, New Jersey

(Top) **Rich Melvin was at the throttle of Nickel Plate 2-8-4 765 as it headed up the New River Gorge on October 16, 1988.**

(Above) **Fireman Tom Stephens handled the coal stoker and water supply to keep NKP 765 right on its 245-psi boiler pressure.**

Virginia & Truckee 2-6-0 No. 13, named *Empire*, is a magnificent example of a post-Civil War steam locomotive. Built by Baldwin in 1873, it carries the typical cinder-bonnet stack of a wood-burner, long pointed "cowcatcher," and large headlight. During this Victorian era, prosperous railroads like the silver-hauling V&T decorated their locomotives in dramatic colors. Her "unlucky" number was changed in 1910 to 15. The *Empire* now resides in this display at the California State Railroad Museum in Sacramento, surrounded by mirrors reminiscent of a Gold Rush bordello.

1

The Early Americans

The age of locomotives began in September 1825 when engine No. 1 of the Stockton & Darlington Railway in England pulled its first passenger train. The *Locomotion* was a wondrous contraption with four driving wheels connected to two vertical cylinders by what looked for all the world like a tangle of coat hangers. This coal-burning machine with a stubby horizontal boiler was built by George Stephenson and his son, Robert, and served the railway until 1858—not a bad career, even by today's standards.

Locomotives gained world wide attention in October 1829 with the seven-day competition in Rainhill, England, to select a locomotive for the then-abuilding Liverpool & Manchester Railway. At the Rainhill Trials, locomotives from different builders were tested side-by-side for power and performance. The winner was the *Rocket*, a four-wheeler with a horizontal boiler and a very tall smokestack; it was the 19th locomotive built by Robert Stephenson & Company of Newcastle. The *Rocket* was the first machine to incorporate the successful elements of horizontal fire-tube boiler, forced draft, and cylinders with rods connecting directly to the driving wheels. During the Trials, the *Rocket* hit 28 MPH—the fastest that man had ever traveled on land up to that time.

From England to America

The idea of railroads came to the New World in the early 1800s, and in 1811 Colonel John Stevens petitioned the New Jersey legislature for a charter to build a railroad, but it would be a few years before Stevens's ambitions could be fulfilled.

Meanwhile, canals were big business, and in 1828 Horatio Allen of the Delaware & Hudson Canal Company ordered a locomotive from Foster,

The *Best Friend of Charleston*, steaming at the Baltimore & Ohio Transportation Museum in Baltimore, Maryland, is an operating replica, since the 1831 original was not only the first American locomotive to enter regular revenue service (January 15, 1831) but also the first to be destroyed in a boiler explosion (June 17, 1831). Most early locomotives like the *Best Friend* were one-of-a-kind machines that were not successful enough to be duplicated.

Forever remembered for losing a race to a real horse, the iron horse *Tom Thumb* was actually a reasonably successful locomotive. In 1977, B&O's *Tom Thumb* replica restaged the horse-race legend at the B&O Railroad Museum.

(Above) A replica of the 1825 British *Locomotion* —the first successful locomotive—was operating at the California State Railroad Museum in 1991. *(Mike Del Vecchio)*

(Right) The *Rocket* beat out the *Locomotion* at the Rainhill Trials in 1829 and was the first locomotive to successfully incorporate a horizontal boiler and drive rods directly linking the cylinders and drive wheels. This static replica of the *Rocket* is on display at the Henry Ford Museum in Dearborn, Michigan.

Rastrick & Company of Stourbridge, England, for his horse-and-gravity tramway which was used to get coal out of Carbondale over a mountain ridge to the canal headwaters at Honesdale, Pennsylvania. The D&H *Stourbridge Lion* became the first locomotive to operate in North America on August 8, 1829. The *Lion* was too heavy and rigid for the crude wood and strap-iron track, however, and never entered revenue service.

One year later, in 1830, the four-wheeled *Tom Thumb,* built by Peter Cooper, carried the directors of the Baltimore & Ohio Railroad 13 miles from Baltimore to Ellicott's Mills in 57 minutes—but went down in history as the locomotive that lost a race with a horse.

On January 15, 1831, the *Best Friend of Charleston,* became the first steam locomotive in America to enter regular revenue service. Built by the West

Point Foundry in New York City, it was operated by the South Carolina Canal & Railroad Company and served successfully until June 17, 1831, when the fireman, irritated by the sound it was making, tied down the safety valve and shortly thereafter became the first American victim of a locomotive boiler explosion.

The *John Bull*

Numerous other one-of-a-kind machines were built and tried with varying degrees of success during this time, but America got its first "real" loco- motive when the *John Bull* arrived by sailing ship at Philadelphia in August 1831. Built and tested by the Stephenson Company in England, it had been disassembled and loaded into great crates for shipment to Col. John Stevens's Camden & Amboy Railroad in New Jersey. When it arrived, a twenty-one-year-old mechanic named Isaac Dripps had the task of reassembling it—hampered by the fact that it had arrived with no plans or instructions and that Dripps had never seen another locomotive and had no idea how it worked or what it should look like when completed! But he had the machine

The original 1831 *John Bull* was restored and operated in 1981 on the B&O's Georgetown Branch near Washington, D.C., to celebrate its 150th birthday as the world's oldest operating self-propelled vehicle. The *John Bull* was even more significant for being the first locomotive that was successful enough to be duplicated in kind.

assembled and operating on September 15, 1831.

The *John Bull* differed from other locomotives of its time in that it had a horizontal fire-tube boiler and two cylinders which drove directly on one of the driving wheel axles. The cylinders exhausted into a smokebox beneath the stack to create a draft. It was the first machine in North America to put together in the right order and proportion all of the elements that we know today comprise a successful steam locomotive.

Originally constructed as an 0-4-0, the *John Bull* had its four 54-inch wooden driving wheels con-

nected by side rods. The Camden & Amboy's shop in Bordentown, New Jersey, modified the locomotive, however, by disconnecting the rods to the front drivers and adding a long wood-beamed "cowcatcher" built as a two-wheel pilot truck. By hanging the cowcatcher off the now-unpowered front drivers, they had created a 4-2-0, which rode surprisingly well on the C&A's primitive track. Modern calculations show that disconnecting the second driver still left the *John Bull* with a perfect "adhesion factor," which meant that the single driver set would pull as great a load as the two sets together.

The *John Bull* was an unqualified success. Over the next six years, no less than 15 more wood-burning locomotives where built to its design in the Bordentown shop with parts both locally manufactured and supplied by Stephenson from England. In September 1833, the Camden & Amboy began regularly scheduled service between South Amboy and Bordentown hauling seven-car trains at speeds up to 30 MPH. Motive power was the *John Bull*-class 4-2-0s, including the original in its proper place as C&A No. 1. It remained in service until retired for preservation in 1866.

The *John Bull* was the first locomotive that was successful enough to be duplicated in kind, forecasting the vast fleets of locomotives that would follow. In 1871 the Pennsylvania Railroad took over the Camden & Amboy, and the PRR knew what a historic gem it had in the *John Bull*. In 1884 the veteran machine became the first engineering specimen in the Smithsonian Institution in Washington, D.C. In 1893, however, it was borrowed back by the PRR and operated under steam on an 1,800-mile round trip to the Columbian Exposition in Chicago. After that, it returned to the Smithsonian and did not operate again until 1980.

On the eve of its 150th birthday, the original *John Bull* was examined by the Smithsonian with the most modern of testing technology and declared suitable for restoration. The *John Bull* performed for the national press on B&O's Georgetown branch near Washington, D.C., on September 15, 1981—150 years to the day after its first test run in America.

The *John Bull* made a number of runs on the Georgetown Branch, being studied and documented on film and videotape by the Smithsonian. The reason for the *John Bull*'s success in 1831 was immediately obvious in 1981. Instead of the timid tick-tocking of the *Tom Thumb* replica, which had operated on its own 150th anniversary in 1980, the *John Bull* had the lusty exhaust and get-up-and-go of a real locomotive. You could easily picture a fleet of these engines operating an entire railroad, day in and day out.

The "American Standard"

The *John Bull* was characteristic of the design and construction that would typify British locomotives. While both the U.S. and Great Britain shared the 4-foot 8^1/$_2$-inch standard-gauge track (derived from Roman chariot roads in England), the railways of the new world took on a much different character from those of the mother country.

In England the railways were constructed into an already densely populated urban countryside, and a fairly restrictive "loading gauge" of side and overhead clearances was adopted for station platforms and bridges. The idea of high-level passenger station platforms was incorporated into British railway design from the onset, and those earth and stone structures crowded the side clearances around the driving wheels of a steam locomotive. As a result, as on the *John Bull*, the British tended to put a locomotive's cylinders under the boiler inside the frames and connect them to cranks on the driving wheel axles.

In America, however, railroads generally were built through open country, and steps on the coaches were far more economical to install than high-level station platforms. As a result, there were no crowded clearances, and when American locomotives grew larger, they simply spread out in all directions, hanging the cylinders and rods outboard of the driving wheels.

In England, the "civilized" railways were fenced, and "level crossings" were kept to a minimum and generally manned with a watchman. In America, they didn't bother to fence the cattle,

(Right) The B&O built a series of 19 "Grasshopper" locomotives between 1832 and 1837. The concept of the vertical boiler and cylinders with "walking beams" was based on the layout of steam-powered water pumps used in coal mines. This engine at the B&O Museum is actually the 1836 *Andrew Jackson,* which was altered in 1892 to resemble the smaller 1832 *Atlantic.* It is one of the oldest existing original locomotives. *(Railfan & Railroad collection)*

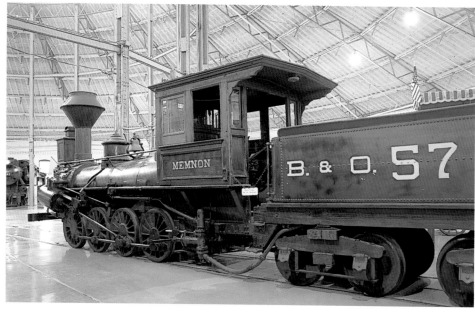

By the 1850s, steam locomotives were rapidly growing in size and power, with horizontal boilers and directly-connected cylinders. B&O's *Memnon,* an 0-8-0 road freight engine built in 1848, illustrates the format.

comfort, the American railroads were flung into the wilderness with only the engineering absolutely necessary for survival. From about 1840 on, American railroads left English engineering behind and went on to develop a style all their own.

From the *John Bull,* locomotives progressed in size and proportion, from the bizarre "Grasshoppers" and utilitarian "Norris" 4-2-0s, like Baltimore & Ohio's *Lafayette,* to the large 0-8-0 "Camels" built by Ross Winans for the B&O. The four-wheel swiveling pilot truck was developed in 1837 and was soon improved with a spring suspension. The resulting 4-4-0 locomotive quickly became the most popular wheel arrangement in the U.S. This "American Standard" placed a narrow firebox between the drivers and extended the boiler forward to rest on a cylinder "saddle" above the four-wheel pilot truck. The arrangement permitted a long open space between the lead driver and the cylinders in which to hang the Stephenson valve gear between the frames. It was easy to maintain, rugged and stable riding on the often crudely graded American track.

much less the railroad tracks. As a result the British railways developed without using headlights or cowcatchers, while the American railroads needed both—as well as lusty whistles and loud bells to warn of their approach. Whereas the British were building well-engineered railroads through cities and villages with bridges and tunnels and rights-of-way designed for speed and

The Mason 4-4-0

The Baltimore & Ohio had bought earlier 4-4-0s, but in 1856 it acquired its first one from William Mason of Taunton, Massachusetts. Whereas the previous 4-4-0s had closely spaced pilot wheels beneath the cylinders, Mason was the first to use a "swing hanger" suspension and spread the pilot wheels apart and place the cylinders between them, lowering the engine's center of gravity and improving both trackworthiness and appearance.

The B&O's first Mason was nameless No. 25, an extraordinarily handsome machine built in November 1856 that forecast the appearance of virtually all the 4-4-0s that would follow for the

(Above) The *Victory* is typical of the earliest 4-4-0s with a rigid center-pivot pilot truck placed directly beneath the cylinders. Most engines with rigid trucks had flanges only on the rear drivers to permit the "blind" front drivers to negotiate curves. (Railfan & Railroad collection)

(Left) William Mason & Company of Taunton, Massachusetts, built No. 25 for the B&O in 1856. It was the first B&O 4-4-0 to use a flexible "swing hanger" pilot truck which rode the track much better than the rigid center-pin types. Mason extended the distance between pilot-truck wheelsets and dropped the cylinders between them, giving the locomotive a lower center of gravity and much-improved appearance. In 1998 the 25 was overhauled and tested on the Strasburg Rail Road for use in the motion picture *Wild, Wild West*.

(Left) The first B&O locomotive with a horizontal boiler was the Norris 4-2-0 *Lafayette*, built in 1837. The center pin of the pilot truck and two driving wheels gave the machine simple but perfect three-point suspension for good riding on crude track. The B&O Museum's *Lafayette* replica is shown at the California State Railroad Museum in 1991.

(Below) Cartoonist and filmmaker Walt Disney was an enthusiastic railroad fan, and one of his first live-action features was *The Great Locomotive Chase*. On location in Georgia in 1955, Walt posed in the cab of the B&O *Lafayette*, which played the heroic switch engine *Yonah* in the movie. *(Railfan & Railroad collection)*

next 20 years. The tall cinder-bonnet stack, long pointed cowcatcher, prominent headlight, sleek cab, and detailed decoration set the pattern for the next generation of "Civil War era" wood-burners.

The B&O was one of the few railroads to take a serious interest in preserving its history, and in 1893 it began collecting and preserving its oldest locomotives that were ultimately housed in the B&O Railroad Museum, which was created from the Mount Clare Shop complex near downtown Baltimore. The main building is the 1884 round-house with its indoor turntable and 22 radial tracks, all under a magnificent domed roof. The entrance is through the world's oldest existing rail-road station, built in 1828.

In 1955 B&O Museum engines starred in the Walt Disney production of *The Great Locomotive Chase*, with 4-4-0 No. 25 (now named *Mason* in honor of its builder) playing the *General* and the Norris 4-2-0 *Lafayette* cast as the heroic switch engine *Yonah*. As recently as 1999, the *Mason* starred in the action movie *Wild, Wild West*.

Although the details would vary, the general size and proportions of the 4-4-0s remained remark-ably unchanged for the next 40 years. These 30-ton machines were the first "dual-service" locomo-tives, equally at home on passenger or freight trains. Still in the era of wood fuel, they were char-acterized by large spark-arresting "diamond" smokestacks; long, pointed cowcatchers; and big, boxy headlights, The driving wheels ranged from 50 to 70 inches in diameter, giving many of them mile-a-minute capability on good track—but good track was often very hard to find.

"American" Movie Stars

The 4-4-0 got America through the Civil War. When Union raiders under the command of James J. Andrews stole a Confederate train at Big Shanty,

Georgia, on April 12, 1862, resulting in the aforementioned *Great Locomotive Chase,* both the stolen *General* and pursuing *Texas* were 4-4-0s. And when they drove the golden spike to complete the first transcontinental railroad on May 10, 1869, both the wood-burning Central Pacific *Jupiter* and nameless, coal-burning Union Pacific No. 119 that met at Promontory Summit, Utah, were 4-4-0s.

Following the Civil War, locomotives were an important part of the American culture, and in that era of gingerbread architecture and Victorian style,

American-type locomotives joined East and West at Promontory, Utah, with the gold spike on May 10, 1869. *(Union Pacific)*

they were often lavishly decorated. At the time it was accepted practice that a crew was assigned to one specific locomotive, and they would often take great care and pride in the engine's appearance.

One of the most outstanding examples of such a locomotive is the Virginia & Truckee 4-4-0 *Inyo.* The V&T of the 1870s was a small but obscenely prosperous railroad that bought the finest locomotives available. Built by Baldwin of Philadelphia in 1875, V&T No. 22 was a 34-ton wood-burning 4-4-0 of classic proportion. Converted to burn oil in 1910, she

A true "American" movie star is the splendidly authentic Virginia & Truckee *Inyo,* built by Baldwin Locomotive Works in 1875. In 1937 the classic 4-4-0 was sold to Paramount Pictures for $1,250 and went on to star in numerous motion pictures and even television shows like the popular series *Wild, Wild West.* Between 1968 and 1979 it played the part of Central Pacific's *Jupiter* at the Golden Spike Historic Site before being sold to the State of Nevada for $75,000 for a new museum in Carson City. In May 1991 the *Inyo* is shown steaming for Railfair at the California State Railroad Museum.

The famous Civil War 4-4-0 *General* was preserved and operated by the Louisville & Nashville Railroad for the centennial of the war. In 1972 it was on display at Big Shanty station in Kennesaw, Georgia, where the 1862 Union raid took place on the Western Atlantic. *(A. M. Langley)*

The typical 4-4-0 was such a utilitarian machine that many had extremely long working lives. This former Tuckerton Railroad 4-4-0 ended up as Southern New Jersey Railroad No. 5. *(L. A. Broomfield, Railfan & Railroad collection)*

spent most of her life working the Nevada silver-mining region until retired in 1926 and put into storage. In 1937 the *Inyo* was sold to Paramount Pictures and spent the next 30 years as a movie star.

The *Inyo* played the part of the *Texas* opposite the B&O *Mason* as the *General* in Disney's *Great Locomotive Chase* and was a regular in the televi-sion series *Wild, Wild West* (the role now played on film by the *Mason*). From 1968 to 1978 the *Inyo* played the part of the Central Pacific *Jupiter* at the Golden Spike National Historic Site and was then sold by Paramount to the State of Nevada for oper-ation at the new Nevada State Railroad Museum in her original home of Carson City.

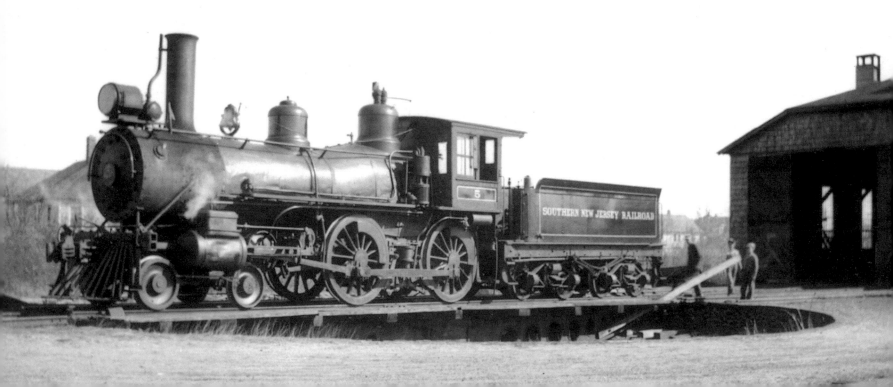

Workaday Americans

By the 1880s, even the 4-4-0s were becoming more workaday machines, and the fancy paint and polished brass detailing was forsaken in the quest for economy. This began the trend toward what we regard as "modern-looking" locomotives. Yet, lack of Victorian splendor did not mean the end to handsome locomotives.

A beautifully-proportioned American Standard of this new era is Denver, Fort Worth & Texas No. 9, built in 1888 by the Cooke Locomotive & Machine Company of Paterson, New Jersey. Originally a coal-burner, this 42-ton 4-4-0 did not need the large cinder-catching stack and spent its entire working career with a tall straight stack. Compared to the Victorian *Inyo*, No. 9 has the look of a more businesslike locomotive.

In 1906 DFtW&T No. 9 settled down as No. 8 of the Dardanelle & Russellville short line in Arkansas. After 34 years on the five-mile-long D&R, No. 8 embarked upon a new career in 1939 as a movie star for 20th Century-Fox, making its debut on the

By the 1900s, railroads had forsaken Victorian decoration for workaday black and numbers instead of names. Knuckle couplers made long cowcatchers impractical, and coal or oil fuel eliminated the need for big cinder-catcher smokestacks. Though built in 1888, Short Line Enterprises oil-burning 4-4-0 No. 8 has a "modern" look at Sacramento in 1981.

Missouri, Kansas & Texas 2-6-0 No. 147 is at McBaine, Missouri, on the "Katy's" St. Louis line in the summer of 1913, ready to take a local freight west to New Franklin. The engineer is going over the running gear in the traditional manner of all good runners. This Mogul-type locomotive was built by Baldwin in 1891 as No. 215 and is typical of the development of the "modern" 2-6-0. (Harold K. Vollrath collection, Railfan & Railroad collection)

silver screen in *Jesse James*. After appearing in numerous films, No. 8 was sold to Short Line Enterprises of Cucamonga, California, which steamed it at the California State Railroad Museum in 1981. Number 8 was subsequently sold to the Nevada State Railroad Museum in Carson City, where it operates today.

Moguls and More

The 4-4-0 was not the only wheel arrangement in common use between the Civil War and the turn of the century, but until the 1880s it was by far the most popular. Similar in size and weight was the 2-6-0 "Mogul" type which can trace its origins back to the 1850s but which became a truly practical locomotive with the development of the

improved "radial" two-wheel pilot truck in 1866.

A magnificent example of an 1873 2-6-0 is the 35-ton Virginia & Truckee No. 13, *Empire*, at the California State Railroad Museum in Sacramento (see page 8). Its brass-bound Victorian splendor is enhanced by its unusual display setting: surrounded top and bottom by mirrors and looking like something out of a Gold Rush bordello!

A logical development of the 4-4-0 was the 4-6-0, and an interesting example of the "Ten-Wheeler" is Clinchfield Railroad No. 1, which was built in August 1882 by the Columbus, Chicago & Indiana Central Railroad shop in Logansport, Indiana, to an 1869 design. The low-slung 4-6-0 migrated to the Carolina, Clinchfield & Ohio in 1900, and in April 1913 it was sold to the 25-mile Black Moun-

Wheel Arrangements

A 4-4-0 of the U.S. Military Railroad, circa 1865. *(Railfan & Railroad collection)*

Steam locomotives are identified by the configuration of their wheels. The North American system counts the actual wheels (two on each axle). In the system devised by Frederick M. Whyte (a New York Central mechanical engineer) and adopted by the American Railway Master Mechanics Association in 1901, the wheel groups are represented by numbers joined with hyphens: thus the Pacific-type locomotive with a four-wheel pilot truck, six drivers, and a two-wheel trailer truck is a 4-6-2. Engines with no pilot or trailer truck simply get zeros in the appropriate slot, with the classic American Standard type being a 4-4-0 and a six-wheel switcher being an 0-6-0. The common verbalization of the zero is "oh." Thus our switcher is an "oh-six-oh." Large locomotives with articulated (hinged) frames and/or additional sets of cylinders get a double number for the drivers, like a 2-6-6-2.

Well before the Whyte system was adopted, it had been common to name locomotive *types* (not to be confused with the naming of individual locomotives), often based upon the first railroad to use the wheel arrangement (the first 4-4-2 Atlantic, for example, was built in 1896 for the Atlantic City Railroad). This tradition continued until the end of steam, and while most type-names were universal, many railroads adopted their own names for specific wheel arrangements. The popular 4-8-4 "Northern" type (named for the Northern Pacific design of 1926) got the greatest variety of individualized names: "Greenbrier" on the Chesapeake & Ohio; "Niagara" on the New York Central and "Pocono" on the Delaware, Lackawanna & Western, to name just a few.

Wheel Arrangement	Name
0-4-0	Switcher
0-6-0	Switcher
0-8-0	Switcher
4-4-0	American
2-6-0	Mogul
4-6-0	Ten-Wheeler
4-8-0	Twelve-Wheeler
2-8-0	Consolidation
2-10-0	Decapod
2-4-2	Columbia
4-4-2	Atlantic
2-6-2	Prairie
4-6-2	Pacific
2-8-2	Mikado
2-10-2	Santa Fe
4-8-2	Mountain
4-10-2	Southern Pacific
4-12-2	Union Pacific
2-8-4	Berkshire
2-10-4	Texas
4-8-4	Northern
4-6-4	Hudson
2-6-6-2	Articulated
2-8-8-2	Articulated
2-8-8-4	Yellowstone
2-6-6-4	Articulated
4-6-6-4	Challenger
2-6-6-6	Allegheny
6-4-4-6	PRR 6100 Duplex
4-4-4-4	PRR T1 Duplex
4-4-6-4	PRR Q2 Duplex
4-8-8-4	Big Boy

21

tain Railroad in North Carolina. When old No. 1 was replaced by a diesel in 1955, it was returned to the Clinchfield for display in Erwin, Tennessee. A friendly Clinchfield management had it back under steam and pulling excursions by 1968.

Watching No. 1 romp through Clinchfield country, you could see a century of history on the move. Though diminutive by latter-day standards of steam and diesel locomotives, No. 1 was clearly capable of mainline performance. After Clinchfield became part of the Seaboard System in 1983 and later CSX, No. 1 went to the B&O Museum.

The 2-6-0s grew into 2-8-0s and even 2-10-0s, as wrought iron and copper was replaced by steel,

and the American industrial revolution provided the manufacturing skills and economic strength to change the railways from pathways in the wilderness to vital arteries binding the nation together. The trackwork was getting better, and the railroads were getting busier. Coal for homes and the industrial furnaces moved from the mines to the cities. Grain and cattle from the West fed the bursting seaboard communities. The railroad was the fastest and most efficient means of overland travel. Not only could trains make "a mile a minute," but by 1897 they had hit the "century mark" of 100 MPH.

And it was just in time to mark a new century.

(Above) Central Pacific 2-6-0 *Hercules* is shown at Cisco, California, in the Sierra in 1868, a year before the completion of the transcontinental railroad. The Mogul-type was built by Danforth, Cooke & Company in 1867 and is typical of the wood-burning 2-6-0s that "won the West" along with the more-numerous 4-4-0s. In fact, this engine was rebuilt into a 4-4-0 by CP and renumbered 13 sometime in the 1870s, and its drivers were increased from 57 to 63 inches, giving it a faster track speed without changing its overall size or power. *(D. L. Joslyn collection, Railfan & Railroad collection)*

(Left) Clinchfield Railroad No. 1 was built in 1882 in the Logansport, Indiana, shop of a predecessor of the Pennsylvania Railroad, to an 1869 design and was sold to the Clinchfield in 1900. After Clinchfield service, it spent many years on a shortline before being placed on display. Number 1 was then overhauled by the Clinchfield at its Erwin, Tennessee, shop and returned to service in 1968 hauling public excursions. Back on the main line, No. 1 scampers southward near Fort Blackmore, Virginia, on May 10, 1969.

Creating the very image of the turn of the century, Pennsylvania Railroad 4-4-2 7002 was making mainline speed through Downingtown, Pennsylvania, on May 18, 1986. On June 12, 1905, the 7002 had set the unofficial world speed record of 127.1 MPH on the *Pennsylvania Special* in Ohio. While this "7002" is actually the sister engine 8063, both were built in the Pennsy's Juniata Shops in 1902 and were for all practical purposes identical. The 8063 was disguised as 7002 by the PRR in 1949 for publicity purposes and was restored by the Pennsylvania State Railroad Museum in 1983. Doubleheaded behind the 7002 is the Strasburg Rail Road's PRR 4-4-0 1223.

Turn of the Century 2

It was more than just bigger locomotives that permitted American railroads to develop into the massive transportation network of the new century. Although all sorts of advances were being made in trackwork and signaling, it was the automatic coupler and air brakes that made possible the trains we know today.

Early coupling devices were generally some type of chain link, and these evolved into the "link-and-pin" couplers that were in widespread use throughout the Civil War era. The first automatic coupler dates from 1848, but the "knuckle coupler" that became standard on American railroads was patented in 1873 by Eli Hamilton Janney. In one simple and rugged mechanism, the Janney coupler could handle both pulling and pushing loads and was operated safely from alongside the car by a long lever.

From the beginning of railroading it had been far easier to start a train than to stop it. As the trains grew longer in the Civil War years, a crew of brakemen would man the hand-operated brakes on each car. In April 1869, New Yorker George Westinghouse patented an automatic braking system operated by compressed air. In 1873 he improved the design so that any break in the "trainline" would cause the brakes to automatically apply. This brake became standard on American railroads, and along with the automatic coupler it made possible the heavy trains of the twentieth century.

The Quest for Speed

In the 1890s America was impressed with speed. Big railroads competed intensely for lucrative passenger business, like giants Pennsylvania Railroad and New York Central with their rival multiple-track main lines between New York and Chicago. By now the 4-4-0 had grown into an impressive mainline machine that was, thanks to good track, routinely capable of mile-a-minute speeds.

It was the knuckle coupler and the automatic air brake that made possible the heavy and fast trains that have typified American railroading for the past century. This coupler can handle both pulling and pushing forces of the train and is operated safely from beside the track instead of between the cars, as was the case with the old link-and-pin system. A modern coupler is shown here on Illinois Central 2-8-0 790 on display in 1960 in Cedar Rapids, Iowa.

On May 10, 1893, a tall-drivered 4-4-0 numbered 999, heading for the Columbian Exposition World's Fair in Chicago, rolled New York Central & Hudson River's *Empire State Express* to the speed of 112.5 MPH near Buffalo, New York. It was the first time any machine had hit the magic 100 MPH mark and was the fastest man had ever traveled and lived to tell about it.

While the 999 made speed news en route to display at the 1893 World's Fair, a much more significant locomotive was already on display there: Baldwin's passenger 2-4-2, which introduced the idea of the trailing truck to permit a larger firebox than was possible with the 4-4-0. Over the next five years this idea resulted in the creation of the 4-4-2, 4-6-2, and 2-8-2-type locomotives that would become the workhorses of the next 30 years.

(Above) The first machine in the world to exceed 100 MPH was New York Central & Hudson River 4-4-0 No. 999 on May 10, 1893. Two years after setting that 112.5 MPH speed record, the 999 is shown on the *Empire State Express*, scooping water from track pans (to reduce the need for water stops). *(Railfan & Railroad collection)*

(Right) The 4-4-0 continued to serve well into the 20th Century as larger and more modern versions were built. Here Jersey Central 547 was departing the huge Jersey City terminal on Dec. 29, 1914, with a short commuter train. *(K.E. Schlachter, Railfan & Railroad collection)*

In 1896 Baldwin built the first 4-4-2 "Atlantic" type for the Atlantic City Railroad, and in 1901 the Pennsylvania Railroad introduced its big Class E2 4-4-2 for fast passenger service. With tall 80-inch drivers and a pair of trailing wheels mounted in the frame beneath the firebox, these engines were designed for speed and power, and by 1914 over 500 had been built.

In 1902 PRR's Juniata Shops in Altoona, Pennsylvania, turned out E2 7002, which on June 12, 1905, turned in the fastest speed run ever claimed for a steam locomotive: 127.1 MPH across Ohio on train No. 29, the *Pennsylvania Special.* Although the proof of this record run is so unscientific that the "official" world steam speed record was later recognized as the carefully-documented 126-MPH performance of the London & North Eastern streamlined 4-6-2 *Mallard* in England in 1938, that didn't stop the Pennsylvania Railroad from publicizing the 7002's record as authentic in 1905.

Central's 999 starred at another celebration in Chicago, the 1948–49 Chicago Railroad Fair where it was displayed as the "first to exceed 100 MPH." Not to be outdone, rival Pennsylvania Railroad went to get its own even faster 7002—only to discover that it had scrapped the engine without ceremony in 1934! However, PRR found sister engine 8063, which had also been built at Juniata in 1902 and overhauled for a display in 1940, only to be set aside at the onset of World War II. When the "7002" went on display for the Railroad Fair's second year, there was no mention that it was actually the 8063.

The PRR was one of the few railroads to have a systematic program of preserving significant examples of its steam locomotives, and the ersatz 7002 was part of the historical collection that in 1979 was donated to the Pennsylvania State Railroad Museum in Strasburg. Although it had been modernized and equipped with superheaters in

Technology was making rapid advances at the turn of the century. Indiana's Purdue University set up an engineering research lab where locomotives could be mounted on rollers and studied "at speed"—though stationary—like this 4-4-0 being tested in 1897. *(O. L. Foster, Railfan & Railroad collection)*

A classic high-drivered 4-4-2, this brand new Cleveland, Cincinnati, Chicago & St. Louis Railroad (the New York Central's "Big Four Route" subsidiary) 373 was wearing its Sunday best for exhibition at the 1904 Universal Exposition in St. Louis. *(H. S. Ludlow, Railfan & Railroad collection)*

Pennsylvania Railroad 4-4-2 7002 set the world speed record of 127.1 MPH in 1905, but this "7002" on the Strasburg Rail Road in 1983 is actually identical sister 8063, renumbered by the PRR in 1949 as a stand-in for the original, which had been scrapped.

1918, the 8063/7002 was authentically restored to a close approximation of its as-built appearance. In 1983, following an overhaul, the "7002" went into regular tourist service on the Strasburg Rail Road.

The 7002 is an excellent and rare image of a turn-of-the-century passenger engine, with her high drivers, inboard-bearing trailer truck, oversize headlight, and delicate pinstriping. In addi-

tion to regular service on the Strasburg, the 7002 made a number of mainline excursions over Amtrak and Conrail lines to Philadelphia and Harrisburg, doubleheaded with the Strasburg's PRR D16sb 4-4-0 No. 1223.

Doubleheaded with a 4-4-0? An example of the ultimate development of her classic wheel arrangement, the 1223 is actually three years

newer than the 8063/7002. Built in 1905 in the Juniata Shop, the 1223 was leased to the Strasburg Rail Road in 1965, where she served over 20 years in tourist service. On the PRR the D16 4-4-0s had survived into the 1950s because they could handle up to six cars on suburban passenger trains, their 68-inch drivers giving them snappy acceleration. Even on the Pennsylvania Railroad, the American was still a useful engine type more than a hundred years after its creation.

A Tale of Two Ten-Wheelers

About the only thing that Warren & Ouachita Valley No. 1 and Chicago & North Western 1385 have in common is their age and 4-6-0 wheel arrangement. The No. 1 sits delicately on the rails, her high headlight a relic of the turn of the century. The 1385 is a massive hulk of a modern locomotive, bulky and businesslike. W&OV No. 1 spent its working life on 16 miles of light rail and sand ballast in the piney woods of Arkansas hauling lumber and woodchips. The 1385, in contrast, had batted commuters at a mile-a-minute down the North Western's three main lines out of Chicago and trundled freight across Midwestern prairies. But both have the "inside" Stephenson valve gear of a Civil War 4-4-0, and they were built within four months of each other!

These two residents of the Mid-Continent Railway Museum in North Freedom, Wisconsin, demonstrate just how different two locomotives of the same era and wheel arrangement can be. Number 1 was built in December 1906 by Baldwin for the W&OV. Intended for light rail and slow speeds, it has the general lines of an older locomotive, with slide valves and its narrow firebox tucked down between the drivers. With 52-inch drivers and a weight of 59 tons, No. 1 was the only one of her kind on the W&OV.

Pennsylvania Railroad Class D16sb 4-4-0 No. 1223 was wheeling through the autumn countryside on the Strasburg Rail Road in October 1980, which was the locomotive's 20th year in tourist service there.

At the age of 32, PRR 1223 was given a complete overhaul and modernized with piston valves at the Juniata Shops in Altoona, where it emerged in freshly painted splendor on May 23, 1937. After starring in the 1939 movie "Broadway Limited," the 1223 and two other D16sb's worked the lines on the Delmarva peninsula until the early 1950s, when it was selected for preservation in the PRR historical collection. *(Railfan & Railroad collection)*

What Makes It "Chug?"

A magnificent plume of "salt and pepper" smoke was being produced by Canadian Pacific 4-6-2s 2317 and 1246 at Steamtown in Bellows Falls, Vermont, in October 1981. The cool air caused the exhaust steam to condense into white billows, while the fireman was "over firing" with coal to produce the unusually heavy black smoke that mixed dramatically with the steam. In regular service, firemen would strive to keep the black smoke to a minimum for both environmental and fuel economy reasons, but they had no control over the white steam.

A locomotive generates steam by heating water with a fire. The boiler is made up of three parts: the firebox, the waist, and the smokebox. Starting in the middle, the waist is simply a big, round tank of water, lying on its side. The smokebox is attached up front, and behind the waist is the firebox. The firebox is an open chamber to hold the fire. It is surrounded by a water jacket on the top, sides, and rear; grates for the fire cover the bottom. To get the fire out of the firebox to heat the water, a series of hollow tubes (flues) runs through the water in the waist. The smokebox is a hollow chamber mounted directly in front of the water-filled portion of the boiler.

The hot gas from the fire heats the water surrounding the firebox and the flues as the gas travels from the grates through the boiler to the smokebox. The smokestack atop the smokebox does more than just provide a hole for the smoke to get out. The stack goes down into the smokebox about half way to the bottom.

Directly beneath the stack is a nozzle for the exhaust steam from the cylinders. As this steam shoots from the nozzle up into the stack, it tends to draw a vacuum within the smokebox that in turn pulls the fire through the flues and air up through the grate in the bottom of the firebox. This intense draft causes the fire to burn hotter and the water to boil faster. Thus, the harder an engine exhausts, the harder it works its fire and—as long as the fuel keeps coming—the harder the locomotive will pull.

After the steam has done its "work" by pushing the piston in the cylinder, it is exhausted on the next stroke into the smokebox and up the stack, creating that characteristic "chug . . . chug . . . chug . . . chug." A conventional two-cylinder locomotive will sound off with four "chugs" for every revolution of the drivers (the chugs come at precisely the 12, 3, 6, and 9 o'clock positions of the rods on the drivers).

As a steam locomotive starts to move, the exhaust sound will at first be loud and slow. As the speed builds up, a "sharpening" of the sound will be the indication that the valve gear lever is being adjusted by the engineer. An overall increase in loudness tells of the throttle being opened further, while a decrease in loudness will indicate the throttle being closed. If you know what you're listening for, you can tell by the sound what the engineer is manipulating in the cab. That's what they mean when they say that a steam locomotive "bares its soul" to the observer.

And what you see coming out of the smokestack is more than just smoke. It is a combination of smoke from the fire plus steam expelled from the cylinders. If a locomotive is being properly fired, there will be very little visible smoke in the hot gasses from the fire. That is why "smoke" from the stack will sometimes be black (when the fire is dirty and the weather warm, where the steam stays invisible) and sometimes pure white (with a clean fire in cold weather, when the steam condenses into magnificent clouds). A smoky fire in cold weather will produce picturesque "salt and pepper" plumes of intermixed pure black smoke and pure white steam.

Although the earliest ones burned wood, modern steam locomotives were fired by either coal or fuel oil—and that choice was largely dependent on a railroad's accessibility to coal. Although some modifications need to be made in the firebox, many locomotives have burned both coal and oil at different times in their service careers (one Shay geared locomotive at the Cass Scenic Railroad in West Virginia was built as a wood-burner, was converted to oil for work in British Columbia, and then later at Cass was converted to coal). The type of fuel to be burned would be specified as a part of the design of a locomotive.

Stripped to its barest essentials during overhaul, this 2-6-0 clearly shows its boiler components: the firebox (left), waist (middle), and smokebox (right), which is centered directly above the cylinders. *(Railfan & Railroad collection)*

This is the inside of a boiler with the flues removed. The steel plate with all the holes is the front flue sheet; beyond is the smokebox. Each hole will hold one end of a steel tube (flue) that carries the fire between the firebox and smokebox. The area where the man is standing is filled with water when the boiler is working. *(Railfan & Railroad collection)*

The 1385 had been built for the C&NW only four months later, in March 1907, by the American Locomotive Company and was one of 275 similar 84-ton R1-class 4-6-0s. The 1385 was obviously intended for mainline work in both freight and passenger service, and her design incorporated piston valves and a wide firebox lifted completely above the drivers. The R-1s proved to be so useful and versatile that they were among the last steam locomotives kept running on the C&NW.

As these two locomotives contentedly haul tourists on Mid-Continent's 4½-mile former-C&NW branch in central Wisconsin, they are living proof that the term "1907 Ten-Wheeler" has relatively little meaning when it comes to defining the size and appearance of a locomotive. By 1907 the problem was no longer just how to make a locomotive bigger—the task was to tailor the locomotive to the job.

Tailored for Freight

While world speed records captured the country's imagination and made newspaper headlines, it was quite likely that the pulpwood from which that newsprint was made and the final rolls of paper for the daily editions were carried from forest to mill to printing plant behind a 2-8-0 freight engine. With its design dating back to the 1860s, over the next half a century the 2-8-0 "Consolidation" became

Here are two 4-6-0s at the Mid-Continent Railway Museum in North Freedom, Wisconsin, that were built within three months of each other for very different railroads. Warren & Ouachita Valley No. 1 (above) was built in December 1905 for use on the fragile track of an Arkansas short line. Chicago & North Western 1385, built by Alco in March 1906, is a much larger mainline machine. Which was the "typical" 1906 Ten-Wheeler?

America's most popular freight locomotive. The name was introduced on the Lehigh Valley Railroad, which had just consolidated a number of smaller railroads to create its system when its first 2-8-0s were delivered.

The earliest 2-8-0s looked like typical Victorian 4-4-0s that had been issued a double ration of driving wheels—complete with diamond stacks, big headlights, and pointed cowcatchers. With nearly all of its weight on its low and powerful drivers and a pilot truck to permit it to ride well at modest speed, the 2-8-0 is just what the railroads needed to keep the industrial revolution rolling. By the turn of the century, the 2-8-0 had developed into an unembellished utilitarian machine with footboards and a small "pilot" replacing the cowcatcher and a road number replacing the name.

Baldwin and the other builders were turning out "standard" 2-8-0s by the hundreds. The customer could specify the general weight and driver diameter and detail package, and Baldwin would crank out a "catalog" 2-8-0 that could be used on a main line or short line.

(Above) At the turn of the century, the 2-8-0 was the most popular type of freight engine in America. Cumberland & Pennsylvania No. 24 was typical of the ones that worked both main lines and shortlines, alike—they just survived longer on shortlines and were replaced on main lines with much larger engines. C&P 24 was photographed in May 1943. *(W. R. Hicks, Railfan & Railroad collection)*

(Left) One of the last 2-8-0s in revenue service was No. 28 of the Duluth & Northeastern, a 12-mile railroad that served paper mills in Cloquet, Minnesota. On June 15, 1963, the 28 had the afternoon run to Saginaw rolling off the bridge at Cloquet. It had been built in 1907 for the Duluth, Missabe & Northern, where it had hauled heavy trains of iron ore.

Superheaters

Water boils at 212 degrees at atmospheric pressure, but when it is trapped within a boiler at around 200 psi, that temperature rises to about 387 degrees—but that steam is still "saturated" with water. It was found that by driving the temperature upward, the steam would "dry out" and become much more efficient. This was accomplished by taking the "wet" steam from the boiler and running it through a series of tubes inside the fire-carrying portion of the boiler flues. By exposing this steam to the hot fire without having any more water available, the steam temperature could be lifted to over 700 degrees. This increased the power and efficiency of the locomotive by as much as 30 percent!

The higher temperature required a better grade of lubricants in the valves and cylinders, and the old slide valves on the cylinders tended to wear quickly when exposed to the hot, dry superheated steam. But by adding superheaters and new piston valves, a railroad could boost the output of an existing locomotive by one-third.

Superheaters were a means of dramatically improving a locomotive's efficiency. On March 30, 1987, the superheater units for Pennsylvania Railroad K4s No. 1361 were on the floor at the Altoona Shops. The upwardly-angled ends are attached to a "header" inside the smokebox after the tubes are inserted inside the larger-diameter fire-carrying flues. Each unit consists of two tubes, so the steam can go down the flue in one tube and return to the front through the other.

Typical Consolidations of the era were two 72-tonners turned out by Baldwin in 1913 for the timber-hauling Duluth & Northeastern in Minnesota. Identical in appearance to C&P 24 on page 33, D&NE 14 and 16 had small 51-inch drivers and Stephenson valve gear. Similar locomotives were in use all across the country, but the two D&NE engines gained fame by sheer survival—they operated in regular freight service until 1963, switching the lumber mills at Cloquet and delivering the traffic to the Duluth, Missabe & Iron Range at Saginaw.

It was about 1901, however, that the 2-8-0 design had begun to evolve into a "modern" locomotive. Up until that time the 2-8-0 still had its narrow firebox tucked between the drivers (like the D&NE 14 and 16), and this severely limited its steaming capacity. By lifting the firebox completely above the drivers, it could be enlarged and made much more efficient. Combined with slightly larger 56-inch drivers, the new firebox design permitted the 2-8-0 to grow into a truly powerful and road-worthy freight engine.

Excellent examples of these "big firebox" 2-8-0s were D&NE's other two road engines, Nos. 27 and 28, that had been built in 1906 and 1907 for the Duluth, Missabe & Northern. The husky 93-ton locomotives that had begun their service lives hauling Missabe iron ore, were sold to the D&NE in

1955. The pair went through some changes in their working life. As built, they operated on 190 pounds of saturated steam. About 1910 a boiler appliance came into general use that was a major technological advance: the "superheater." Both of the DM&N engines had received superheaters in the 1920s and survived into the 1960s as useful, modern locomotives. Ironically, the modern-looking 27 and 28 were actually the older of the D&NE 2-8-0s, as the little saturated 14 and 16 were seven years newer!

All the D&NE engines were retired in 1964 and put on display: the 14 at Hill City, South Dakota; the 16 and 27 in their hometown of Cloquet; and the 28 at the Lake Superior Transportation Museum in Duluth.

The Green Mikado

While 2-8-0s were being built by the thousands during the first decade of the twentieth century, the first 2-8-2 had been created by Baldwin in 1897 for an export to Japan (whose emperor was known as the "Mikado"). By moving the firebox completely behind the drivers, Baldwin had created a locomotive with a much wider and longer firebox than had been possible even on the big 2-8-0s—and a bigger firebox would permit a larger and more efficient boiler.

In October 1911 the Southern Railway bought its

The first 2-8-2 was built in 1897 for export to Japan, and the type was named "Mikado" in honor of the Japanese emperor (during World War II they were often referred to by a new, more politically correct term "MacArthurs"). By placing the big firebox completely behind the drivers and supporting it with a two-wheel trailing truck, the 2-8-2 could achieve much greater power than a 2-8-0, and the Mikado grew rapidly in size. Milwaukee Road 8662 is a USRA Heavy Mikado, built by Alco under government order in 1918. *(Milwaukee Road Historical Association)*

The Southern Railway's first Mikado, No. 4501, was built by Baldwin in October 1911 and sold in October 1948 to the Kentucky & Tennessee where, as K&T No. 12, it became the biggest locomotive ever to run on that ten-mile coal-hauling shortline. On November 8, 1963, the grimy black No. 12 was working a train-load of coal uphill from the mine at Oz to the Southern Railway inter-change at Stearns, Kentucky. One year later, No. 12 was sold to Paul H. Merriman and went on to a career as one of the most famous restored steam locomotives in America as Southern "Green Mikado" 4501. (John J. Wheelihan)

first 2-8-2 from the Baldwin Locomotive Works. The 136-ton 4501 was a big locomotive for her day. Her 63-inch drivers gave her good speed, and she was built with superheaters, piston valves, and Walschaerts valve gear. The 4501 and her 24 sisters had long careers on the Southern and were supplemented by even bigger 2-8-2s.

The 4501 became a survivor when she was sold in October 1948 for $8,225 to the 10-mile Kentucky & Tennessee at Stearns, Kentucky, where it was the biggest locomotive ever to run on the shortline. For the next 16 years No. 12 would haul endless loads of coal uphill from the mine at Oz to the Southern interchange at Stearns.

Three diesel switchers rendered No. 12 surplus in 1964, and Southern's first Mikado was then purchased for $5000 by Paul H. Merriman, an electronics engineer for DuPont and a man with a love of Southern Railway steam. Mr. Merriman prevailed upon the hard-nosed Southern to let him

(Top) Kentucky & Tennessee No. 12 was overhauled by Paul Merriman in 1965 and returned to service in 1966 as the green-and-gold Southern 4501. It is shown in June 1967 heading up an excursion train between Cincinnati, Ohio, and Lexington, Kentucky. The livery is based upon Southern's famous Virginia green that had been applied to its passenger locomotives since 1925 when its President Fairfax Harrison was inspired by the London & North Eastern's green locomotives in England (see the *Flying Scotsman* on page 122). The only surviving authentic green Southern locomotive is the classic Ps4-class Pacific 1401 *(above)*, enshrined at the Smithsonian Institution in Washington, D.C. Although the 4501 had worked its career on the Southern painted in freight black, it was to spend most of its post-retirement years as a passenger engine and therefore was given the green-and-gold livery.

move the 4501 home to Chattanooga under steam. For the next two years she underwent a total overhaul at the Tennessee Valley Railroad Museum and emerged in the Virginia green and gold that Merriman had remembered on Southern passenger locomotives from his college days.

The 4501 had succumbed to the "I wanna be a Ps4" syndrome. In the 1920s, the Southern had a grand fleet of passenger engines, most notably the Class Ps4 Pacifics (4-6-2s), that were legendary for their striking Virginia green boilers with gold trim. Only one Ps4 survives, the 1401, permanently displayed within an exhibit hall at the Smithsonian Institution in Washington, D.C. With a Ps4 thus forever out of reach, every former-

The "Big Four Route" of the New York Central System bought 50 straight-boilered light Pacifics from Brooks and Schenectady between 1905 and 1915. Weighing 104 tons and riding on 75-inch drivers, the 6412 was slightly larger than the Florida East Coast 4-6-2s, which had 69-inch drivers and were two tons lighter. *(Thomas Taber, Railfan & Railroad collection)*

Southern locomotive to pull passengers in recent years has run the risk of getting the green paint.

As the 4501 emerged after restoration, Southern's Vice President–Law, W. Graham Claytor Jr., became the spokesman for the locomotive within the corporate hierarchy, and while Graham's boss, the totally tough and modern President D. W.

Savannah & Atlanta 750 began life in 1910 as Florida East Coast No. 80, the first of a large fleet of light but fast 4-6-2s. It was preserved by the Atlanta Chapter of the National Railway Historical Society and became part of Southern Railway's steam excursion program under SR President W. Graham Claytor Jr. In July 1983 the 750 heads northbound through Orange, Virginia, en route from Charlottesville to Alexandria. These FEC Pacifics were typical of pre-World War I mainline passenger locomotives.

Brosnan, ran one of the most efficient railroads in the country, he knew that his company could use a public relations dose of "Southern" hospitality. In August 1966 the 4501 steamed an excursion up the Southern from Chattanooga to Richmond, Virginia, and one of the longest running corporately sponsored steam programs was under way. Graham Claytor succeeded Mr. Brosnan as president of the company, and steam was home to stay.

Florida East Coast Pacifics

Sharing the Southern Railway steam program in the 1970s with Mikado 4501 was a trim little 4-6-2 dressed up as Savannah & Atlanta 750. The Mikado and Pacific were both developed in the late 1890s,

but it wasn't until the early twentieth century that they realized their potential. The 4-6-2 and 2-8-2 were alter egos of the same locomotive. The four-wheel pilot truck and six tall drivers made the Pacific a passenger engine, while the four lower drivers and a two-wheel pilot truck of a Mikado would fit into the same space under the boiler, to make a freight engine. In later years, many railroads—especially the Pennsylvania—used the same boiler for both their 2-8-2s and 4-6-2s.

Built by Alco's Schenectady Works in January 1910, S&A 750 had begun life as No. 80, the first of a large fleet of light 4-6-2s for the Florida East Coast Railway, which by 1912 linked Jacksonville and Miami with Key West on Henry Flagler's famous

Though it appears quite different with its high headlight, Whippany River 148 is an identical sister to S&A 750 (bottom, opposite), as both came from the Florida East Coast. The 148 closely resembles how the engines looked on the FEC. The light Pacific was rounding "Collins Curve" on the old Erie Railroad four-track main line at Waldwick, New Jersey, in September 1975 for a Ridgewood "Railroad Days" celebration.

"railroad that went to sea" on long bridges far out over ocean waters. Since the line was essentially sea-level flat, the 102-ton 4-6-2s could handle six-car passenger trains at 60-MPH speeds. The FEC must have liked her design, for construction of similar engines continued through 1922.

The FEC didn't fare well in the Depression, however, and No. 80 was sold in 1935 to the Savannah & Atlanta. The S&A wound up as part of the Southern Railway, and in 1962 the 750 was donated to the Atlanta Chapter of the National Railway Historical Society. This fine example of an early Pacific soon joined Southern's steam excursion fleet. The 750's appearance had been considerably altered during her S&A years. She had been built as an oil burner, but the S&A had converted her to coal. In

addition, her high headlight was repositioned on the smokebox front with the bell hung out on top in a more typical Southern Railway treatment.

Interestingly, three other members of her FEC class were restored for operation: the 113 and 153 at the Gold Coast Railroad Museum in Miami and the 148 on two different tourist railroads in New Jersey. The 113, 153, and 148 had all been sold by the FEC to the U.S. Sugar Corporation for use at its mill in Clewiston, Florida.

The 750 and 148 are superb examples of early 4-6-2s that were mainline locomotives in the era of wooden passenger cars, and they also demonstrate how different identical locomotives can look when their "details" like headlight, bell, and tenders are changed.

Relettered Norfolk & Western for the occasion, Strasburg Rail Road's ex-N&W 4-8-0 475 was powering a mixed train for photographers on June 30, 1995, during the annual convention of the National Railway Historical Society in nearby Lancaster, Pennsylvania. When they were new in 1906, these 4-8-0s were the biggest and most powerful locomotives on the entire N&W system.

N&W 4-8-0s

That first decade of the twentieth century was a fascinating one as each railroad looked at the technological advances in a different way. The Norfolk & Western was lugging hoppers out of the hollows and carrying coal to tidewater behind more than 450 2-8-0s, which weren't quite up to the job. The N&W needed raw pulling power more than speed, and the new Mikado seemed to waste too much of its weight on a non-productive trailing truck when it could be holding the drivers to the rail.

The N&W's idea of a better locomotive was essentially one with the same 56-inch drivers as the 88-ton 2-8-0s but with a bigger boiler. What they came up with was a 4-8-0, with the heavy firebox riding atop the drivers and the smokebox extended forward over a four-wheel pilot truck. The 4-8-0 Twelve-Wheeler (also called a "Mastodon") dated back to the 1860s but was not a particularly common configuration.

In 1906 and 1907 the N&W took delivery of 125 Class M 4-8-0s, and the 100-ton "Mollies" were immediately the biggest and heaviest locomotives on the railroad. They were an odd mix of old and new, having traditional inside valve gear but

improved piston valves. The superheater was still a few years in the future, and the M's were all built as saturated-steam engines.

The 4-8-0s were unusual in that they were "deckless" locomotives. To effectively distribute the boiler's weight on the drivers, the firebox was moved completely to the rear of the frame, and the cab was mounted atop the firebox, rather than behind it. The engineer operated the locomotive from a narrow compartment beside the firebox, sitting on a drop-down seat. The firedoor stuck out the back of the cab, and the fireman stood on the front of the tender to shovel the coal—an arrangement similar to Camelback locomotives with their double cabs.

The N&W was happy with the new 4-8-0s and over the next few years continued to build bigger and more powerful versions of the wheel arrangement. Their rein on the main line was short-lived, however, when the first 2-6-6-2 compound articulateds (see next topic) arrived in 1912 and were augmented by huge 2-8-8-2s in 1918. The 4-8-0s soon found themselves relegated to branch lines, locals and yard jobs. In 1915 a few were superheated, and in the 1930s some were equipped with modern

Around the turn of the century, builders were seeking ways to make steam locomotives more powerful and efficient. One approach was compounding, where the steam was used twice. Hot steam from the boiler was sent directly into a small high-pressure cylinder and then exhausted into a larger low-pressure cylinder to be used again. On Southern Pacific 4-4-2 3017, built by Baldwin in 1903 with 79-inch drivers, the high-pressure cylinders were 15 inches in diameter, while the low-pressure ones were 25 inches. This particular engine normally was assigned to service between Oakland and Sacramento, California, and was scrapped during the World War I, when superheaters proved to be much more efficient with much less mechanical complexity. *(Railfan & Railroad collection)*

The "Lindbergh Atlantic"

The Pennsylvania State Railroad Museum had Pennsy E6s Atlantic 460, K4s 3750, and GG1 electric No. 4800 lined up for a night photo session for the NRHS 50th anniversary convention on August 22, 1986. The locomotives had their lights illuminated, and smoke was provided to make the 460 appear to be alive under steam.

The "Lindbergh Atlantic" 460 had a long life on branchline passenger service between Camden and Cape May, New Jersey. It is shown at Pemberton in 1955. *(Homer R. Hill)*

The Pennsylvania Railroad had gotten its first 4-6-2 in 1904 and was operating 259 of them before it rolled out the first K4s in 1914. But in 1910 the Pennsy had made an unusual step backwards in wheel arrangements by returning to the 4-4-2 for further development. By placing a hefty boiler atop two sets of 80-inch drivers they came up with an economical locomotive that on a flat railroad could match the performance of the 4-6-2s of the day. They built a single E6-class Atlantic in 1910, and after four years of experiments and testing two more prototypes, the Pennsy committed to 80 of the superheated E6s version, all built by Juniata Shop in 1914. The E6s proved to be a potent little speedster that remained in fast service on short passenger trains right up to the end of steam.

The boiler used on the E6s Atlantic was actually designed in 1908 for the H8 2-8-0. With 62-inch drivers, the 2-8-0s were limited to 50 MPH, but they were excellent freight engines, and before production was completed in 1916, the Pennsy owned 1,206 of them.

The superheated H10s/E6s boiler was so successful, that it was used again in 1923 for the Class G5s 4-6-0s. Riding on 68-inch drivers, the G5s's were turned out by Altoona between 1923 and 1925 and were the heaviest 4-6-0s ever built. While they saw extensive service on the PRR and were noted for their snappy acceleration, they gained fame as the dominant locomotive hauling commuters on the Long Island Rail Road, which operated 31 engines built by Juniata in 1928. The same boiler on 1206 2-8-0s, 121 4-6-0s, and 83 4-4-2s—now that was standardization!

Undoubtedly the most famous of the E6s 4-4-2s was the "Lindbergh Engine," No. 460. When Charles Lindbergh made his triumphant return to America after becoming the first person to fly solo across the Atlantic Ocean in 1927, there was an intense competition among the movie theaters on New York's Broadway to be the first to show newsreel films of his arrival in Washington, D.C. In the new "aviation

The Pennsylvania Railroad owned 1,206 nearly identical 2-8-0s in the H8, H9, and H10-classes. H10s-class 7688 is shown at the Pennsylvania State Railroad Museum in 1994.

age," everyone was trying to hire the fastest airplane to fly the film to New York, where it could be processed and sped to the awaiting screens.

Everyone, that is, except one theater owner, who set up a film processing lab in a Pennsy baggage car and developed the film en route as 4-4-2 460 dashed the 216 miles from Washington to Manhattan Transfer in 175 minutes, averaging 74 MPH. The film that traveled by rail was on the Broadway screen long before the film that had gone by plane!

The 460 wound out her career in fast passenger service to Atlantic City and Cape May, New Jersey, and is today on display at the Pennsylvania State Railroad Museum in Strasburg along with H10s 2-8-0 7688 and G5s 4-6-0 5741—three identical boilers and one legend.

The E6 4-4-2s and H8–H10 2-8-0s were designed around 1910 using the same boiler. In 1923 the PRR used that same boiler again for a heavy 4-6-0 for commuter service on both the PRR (90 engines) and its subsidiary Long Island Rail Road (31 engines). The comparatively small 68-inch drivers gave the G5s's snappy acceleration and good power. Long Island G5s 35 is wheeling along at Syosset, New York, in 1950. (Ron Ziel collection)

Baltimore & Ohio's 2400 of 1903, a compound 0-6-6-0 known as "Old Maude," was North America's first "Mallet articulated" with two sets of cylinders and drivers linked by a hinge in the underframe. The boiler and firebox sat rigidly upon the rear "engine," while the front engine was hinged at the rear and could swing from side to side at the front to negotiate curves. With small drivers and no pilot truck, this locomotive was designed for low-speed pusher service on steep grades. Note the modern round piston valves on the rear high pressure cylinders and the older square slide valves on the low pressure (and lower steam temperature) front cylinders. *(Railfan & Railroad collection)*

Baker valve gear. The Depression saw the fleet drastically reduced, but those 4-8-0s that survived generally went on to long and productive careers. A few of those Class M's gained fame by handling mixed trains on the picturesque Blacksburg and Abingdon branches right to the end of steam.

Although the 433 is "stuffed and mounted" on display alongside her now-abandoned branch line at Abingdon, Virginia, one Blacksburg veteran survives in operation today. The 475 went through many owners before coming into the capable hands of the Strasburg Rail Road in Pennsylvania in 1991. Steaming gently in the Pennsylvania Dutch countryside, it's hard to imagine this delicate machine as "the biggest locomotive ever" on the N&W in 1907!

The Missing Links

There were some locomotives developed around 1900 for which few examples remain today. These "missing links" seldom survived the Great Depression of the 1930s because by that time they had either become obsolete, worn out, or modernized. Among these were early compounds.

In an effort to gain greater efficiency from a saturated-steam locomotive, the concept of "compound" cylinders was introduced in the 1880s. It

was known that steam still possessed considerable heat energy even after being exhausted from a cylinder, and capturing this steam and re-using it in another cylinder would make the locomotive more efficient. This *compound* use of steam saw many variations, but only one—the compound articulated—was successful enough to warrant continued use and development.

The basic idea of a compound was to use the steam direct from the boiler in a relatively small high-pressure cylinder and then route its exhaust steam into a much larger low-pressure cylinder. By making the low-pressure cylinder about two-and-one-half times larger in diameter than the high-pressure cylinder, both would exert nearly identical thrust on the driving rods—and since the fuel created the steam only once, this double use increased the locomotive's power and efficiency without increasing fuel cost. Most compounds were mechanically complex and ultimately were rendered obsolete by the use of superheaters. By the 1930s, most early compounds had been rebuilt with superheaters and conventional cylinders.

Compound Articulateds

The one area where compounding was an unquestioned success, however, was on articulated loco-

(Above) The 80-mile coal-hauling Interstate Railroad of Andover, Virginia, bought two new 2-8-8-2 compound articulateds from Alco in 1923. Number 20 is shown at Norton, Virginia, on August 9, 1947. (August A. Theime, Railfan & Railroad collection)

(Left) The last new steam locomotive built by Baldwin for a domestic customer was Chesapeake & Ohio 1309 in September 1949, a World War I-era compound 2-6-6-2, now at the B&O Museum.

Slow but powerful, Reading compound 2-8-8-0 1624 was using its steam twice as it hauled hoppers into Pottsville Junction, Pennsylvania, on May 11, 1947. *(C. W. Jernstrom, Railfan & Railroad collection)*

motives. By 1900 it was becoming obvious that more than ten drivers (five axles) would be difficult in navigating curves, and this limited the growth potential of the locomotive. In 1888 a Swiss designer named Anatole Mallet had produced a locomotive with a hinge in its underframe and two sets of cylinders and drivers. In 1903 Alco built the first "Mallet" in North America for the Baltimore & Ohio. An 0-6-6-0, "Old Maude" had her high pres-

sure cylinders on the rear set of six drivers and the big low pressure cylinders on the front set. The boiler was attached to the rear frame, while the front frame was hinged forward from the rear set of cylinders and was able to swing side-to-side at the front. The weight of the boiler was transferred to the front frame by a sliding bracket beneath the smokebox. This entire front frame (known as the "lead engine") had a centering device to aid in

keeping the locomotive stable. Most early articulateds were low-drivered machines intended for great power at low speed.

The terms "compound" and "articulated" actually mean two different things: "Compound" describes the second cylinders to re-use the steam, while "articulated" refers to the hinged frame. There were many compound locomotives that were not articulated and later many articulateds that were not compound. In American terminology, only a compound articulated is referred to as a Mallet (with "MAL-ley," like "valley," being the most common pronunciation).

With the creation of a compound 2-6-6-2 for the Great Northern in 1906, the Mallet had become an accepted concept for a main line locomotive. In fact, the very last new steam locomotive built by Baldwin for a U.S. customer was Chesapeake & Ohio 1309, a compound 2-6-6-2 delivered in September 1949 (it is today at the B&O Museum).

By the end of the first decade of the twentieth century, the American steam locomotive had come of age. With good steel and manufacturing technology and a rapidly-expanding understanding of the physics of steam and potential of locomotive design, the next advances would be simply in size and efficiency.

But those advances would be awesome!

Long after most roads had given up on the compound articulated as being too slow, Norfolk & Western was continuing into 1952 to build its Y6b's, based on the USRA Heavy 2-8-8-2 but modernized with cast engine beds, roller bearings, and advanced lubrication. At the Boaz helper pocket near Roanoke, Virginia, in 1958, two Y6's await helper duty on the Blue Ridge grade as another Y6 eases in with an upbound coal train. *(Jim Shaughnessy)*

The Standard Era

By 1914 America had developed the technology to build what we would recognize as "modern" locomotives. There were three big commercial builders (Baldwin, Alco, and Lima) plus numerous railroad shops which were constructing complete locomotives. Probably the most important of the home shops was the Juniata (JOON-ee-AH-ta) Works of the Pennsylvania Railroad in Altoona, and one of its finest products was the famous Class K4s 4-6-2. The PRR at that time comprised an estimated ten percent of American railroading (one out of ten of everything—locomotives, miles of track, employees, dollars—in the entire industry belonged to the PRR). It was also one of the first railroads to develop truly "standard" equipment, and in 1914 it was creating two locomotives, a freight 2-8-2 and a passenger 4-6-2, using one standard boiler. To say that they were successful is one of the great understatements in railroading: Over the next 14 years 574 L1s Mikados and 425 K4s Pacifics were built to that standard design.

The term "standard" as applied to the PRR was typical of the railroad industry of that time— "standard" meant standard on "my" railroad only. The Pennsy locomotives were quite unlike anything that could be found on other railroads in both appearance and engineering. For example, the PRR was one of the few railroads to wholeheartedly embrace the Belpaire firebox, with its box-like top construction that substantially reduced the number of potentially-troublesome staybolts in the boiler. For a railroad that claimed the title "The Standard Railroad of the World," the good ol' Pennsy was about as non-standard as you could get!

The prototype K4s, 1737, was built at Juniata in May of 1914. With 80-inch drivers, 205 pounds of

(Above) This sunset marked the beginning of a new life for Pennsylvania Railroad K4s 1361, as it rolled out of Altoona Car Shop under steam for the first time since its overhaul on April 11, 1987.

(Facing page) Built in 1923, Chicago, Burlington & Quincy 2-8-2 4960 was kept in service well into the 1960s by "Q" president Harry Murphy for excursions, like this mid-week special for local school children. It is crossing the Illinois Central at Mendota, Illinois, as the engineer prepares to grab train orders from the tower operator.

Forever locked behind a fence—or so most thought—PRR K4s 1361 stands silent at Horseshoe Curve near Altoona, Pennsylvania, in 1969 as a Penn Central freight drifts by. Less than 20 years later, the distinctively Pennsy 4-6-2 would be alive and well while an Electro-Motive GP9 diesel would stand in its place behind the fence! *(Mike Schafer)*

(Above) The resurrection: After its removal from Horseshoe Curve, K4s 1361 undergoes overhaul in Conrail's Altoona Car Shop by Doyle McCormack's crew in March 1987.

(Right) Designed in 1914 and produced until 1928 to total a fleet of 425 identical locomotives, the K4s was the very symbol of the mighty Pennsylvania Railroad in the Standard Era. Over the years the speedy K4s's were modernized and lasted until the very end of steam. In 1956 K4s 612 was accelerating smartly out of South Amboy, New Jersey, with a commuter train. The rectangular box beneath the headlight is a modern front-end throttle applied to a few K4s's. *(Homer R. Hill)*

50

(Left) The "alter ego" of the racy K4s was the workaday L1s 2-8-2, as both locomotives were designed in 1914 to utilize the same boiler and many other common elements. The PRR favored the "Belpaire" firebox with its square "shoulders," which simplified internal construction. The only survivor of the PRR's 574 L1s Mikados is the 520, shown here on May 18, 1991, at the Pennsylvania State Railroad Museum in Strasburg.

(Below) Compare the details of K4s 1361 and L1s 520. On September 16, 1988, the 1361 is shown making short trips for the Railroaders' Memorial Museum between Altoona and Duncansville on the Holidaysburg branch. The images were classic Pennsy beneath the rainy skies.

boiler pressure, and superheaters (hence the "s" in K4s), the K4s passenger engines were excellent machines that incorporated a few modern elements (one-piece cast trailing truck and a combustion chamber inside the boiler) with a solid, basic design that could be upgraded over the years—the first K4s's were hand-fired and had a screw-type manual reverse gear, which were later replaced with mechanical stokers and a power reverse. The addition of mechanical stokers was a radical departure for the PRR, which had always felt that the best stokers in the world were produced by the mothers of Altoona.

The K4s immediately became the mainstay of the PRR passenger fleet, heading up the biggest and most prestigious trains. Even by the 1940s when they had to doubleheaded on the heavier trains, the K4s's were never completely replaced until diesels took over.

Today, one L1 and two K4s's survive. The State Railroad Museum of Pennsylvania has on static display L1s 520 and K4s 3750. The other K4s, the 1361, was placed on display in 1957 at the famous Horseshoe Curve in the mountains west of Altoona. In 1985 she was removed with the cooperation of Conrail and taken to Altoona and was restored to service in April 1987 at Juniata Shops by a crew from the Railroaders Memorial Museum of Altoona. The 1361's display track on Horseshoe Curve is now occupied by a GP9 diesel!

The USRA Standards

While the Pennsy was practicing its own style of standardization, America was dragged into the First World War in April 1917, and by the following winter the North American railroad systems were being severely stressed by the sudden burden of wartime traffic. In the name of the war emergency, the United States Railroad Administration (USRA)

was created in January 1918 to take over the operation of the American rail network. As part of its authorizing legislation, the USRA had a mandate to create a series of standard locomotive designs that could be used anywhere in the country. This idea of standardization was greeted with hostility by the railroad industry, as each company considered its needs to be unique. The Pennsy and New York Central operating the same locomotive? Unthinkable!

Undaunted by the outcry, the USRA assembled a blue-ribbon team of designers from the locomotive manufacturers, headed by the highly-respected Samuel Vauclain of Baldwin. By the end of April 1918—within only four months—the committee submitted 12 standard designs that were the state of the art of the time. Before the railroads were returned to private ownership following the

B&O 4500, built by Baldwin in 1918, was the very first locomotive built to a USRA design during World War I. The Light Mikado was on display at the B&O Museum in Baltimore, where the heating plant's exhaust steam was piped out of the 4500's smokestack to make it appear to be under steam. In an era when every railroad was fiercely independent about designing its own locomotives, it is amazing that the standard USRA designs were widely accepted. There were 1,856 USRA locomotives built under government order and 3,251 copies after the war for 97 different railroads!

(Above) Pittsburgh & Lake Erie 8000 is very clearly recognizable as a USRA standard 0-8-0 switcher, but it was built by Lima in 1937, 17 years after the USRA ceased to exist! Nearly every switch engine built after 1920 was based on a USRA design. (Lima Locomotive Works, Railfan & Railroad collection)

(Right center) Louisville & Nashville 278, built by Brooks in 1924, was a copy of a USRA Light Pacific; it is shown at Louisville in 1952. Although details often varied from one railroad to another, USRA engines were usually easy to identify. (Vitaly V. Uzoff, Railfan & Railroad collection)

(Right bottom) Chicagoan Dick Jensen bought Grand Trunk Western USRA Light Pacific 5629 and operated it out of Chicago in the 1960s. On October 30, 1966, it is riding the turntable at the C&WI 47th Street roundhouse prior to backing to Dearborn Station to take an excursion over the GTW to South Bend, Indiana.

The 83-mile Lehigh & Hudson River Railroad was assigned four Light Mikados by the USRA in 1918, Nos. 80–83. In early 1941 the 83 doubleheads uphill out of Andover to Port Morris, New Jersey, on the Delaware, Lackawanna & Western Sussex branch with the midday train out of Maybrook, New York. The DL&W had sent a heavy 2-8-2 to the L&HR junction at Andover to work as a helper up the hill to Cranberry Lake, and since it was facing north, it was cut in behind the L&HR engine and doubleheaded to Port Morris running backward. L&HR 83 has the classic "USRA look," although the feedwater pump on the pilot deck was added in later years. *(Robert F. Collins)*

(Above) Dick Jensen's USRA 4-6-2 5629 crosses the old Nickel Plate at East Wayne interlocking, Valparaiso, Indiana, on October 30, 1966, bound for South Bend on the GTW.

(Right) Later that same day, the 5629 speeds toward South Bend. The 5629 was a USRA copy built by Alco in 1924 with a modern cast "Delta" trailing truck (compare with L&N 278 on page 54). To get a greater "range," Jensen replaced 5629's original small tender with a large one off a Soo Line 4-8-2.

war in 1920, a total of 1,856 "government" engines had been built—but these locomotives were so well designed, that 3,251 more "copies" were built on order from the railroads themselves after the war. The idea of standardization had obviously won some converts.

The 12 USRA designs were an 0-6-0, an 0-8-0, "Light" and "Heavy" versions each of the 2-8-2, 4-6-2, 4-8-2 and 2-10-2, as well as a compound 2-6-6-2 and 2-8-8-2. These were all superheated and equipped with as many common design elements as possible. And, indeed, the arch-rival PRR and NYC both ended up owning USRA Light Mikados (84 on the NYC and five on the PRR).

A number of USRA engines have been preserved. There are two C&O "copy" 2-6-6-2s (the last new steam locomotives built by Baldwin for U.S. use) in existence, and a Duluth, Missabe & Northern Light 2-10-2 at the National Railroad Museum in Green Bay, Wisconsin, for instance, as well as a few Light 2-8-2s and 4-6-2s in various places, including

B&O Light 2-8-2 4500 at the Baltimore museum, the very first USRA locomotive built.

Only three USRA road engines have been restored for operation, and two are from the same railroad: the Grand Trunk Western, a U.S. subsidiary of the Canadian National. Light Pacific 5629 was a USRA copy built by Alco in 1924 for mainline passenger service. Being a postwar copy, she differed in some details from the government engines, such as in having a modern "Delta" trailing-truck casting. She was sold in 1960 to Chicagoan Dick Jensen and in 1965 became one of the very first privately owned steam locomotives to operate on mainline railroads (B&O and GTW).

In 1969 Dick Jensen overhauled GTW USRA Light 2-8-2 4070, which had been built as a government original in December 1919. She had been sold by GTW in 1961 and changed hands a couple of times before becoming the property in 1968 of the Midwest Railway Historical Foundation of Cleveland, Ohio. In 1975 the 4070 became the regular power on the Cuyahoga Valley Line tourist run

(Above) Grand trunk Western Light Mikado 4070 is operating on the Cuyahoga Valley Line tourist railroad on September 23, 1979, as it eases through Cleveland's industrial bottomlands to its home at B&O's Clark Avenue roundhouse.

(Left) Earlier that same day, the 4070 had the northbound tourist train passing beneath the Ohio Turnpike bridges over the Cuyahoga River valley. The train operates on the B&O Akron–Cleveland branch. The 4070 is a USRA original, built in 1918 as GTW 474 and modified in 1925 with its smokebox extended to accommodate an internal Coffin feedwater heater.

59

on a 26-mile former-B&O line that follows the Cuyahoga River to Akron, Ohio.

The 5629, however, did not meet so kind a fate. As an "ordinary working man," Dick Jensen could no longer afford to maintain or pay storage on his locomotive after he was injured in a non-railroad-related accident, and the 5629 was scrapped in July 1987 in Blue Island, Illinois, in spite of numerous efforts to save her.

In 1987 another original USRA 2-8-2 was restored to service. Nickel Plate 587 had been built in 1918 as Lake Erie & Western 5541 and became NKP 587 in 1924. It was donated in 1955 to the City of Indianapolis, Indiana. After display in a city park, the 587 was pulled out in 1984 and overhauled by a local volunteer group. In 1934 the Nickel Plate had equipped many of its USRA Light Mikados with very large tenders, and the 587 was given one of those just prior to its retirement. That huge tank comes in very handy in today's dieselized world. The 587 now resides at the Indiana Transportation Museum in Noblesville.

(Above) In spite of intense efforts to save it, GTW 5629 was cut up for scrap when Dick Jensen could not pay long overdue storage bills. Since it was in no condition to be moved, the 5629 was cut up on the spot at Blue Island, Illinois, to make room for an intermodal terminal. On July 18, 1987, the scrappers had cut away the top of the boiler, clearly showing its internal construction. The front flue sheet is standing with the superheater header and steam pipes to the cylinders. The worker is standing atop a few remaining flues still attached to the rear flue sheet, where others had been cut away; the larger-diameter flues contained the superheaters. The porcupine-like rods are the radial staybolts that connect the crown sheet over the firebox to the outer boiler shell. *(Patrick Golden)*

(Right) Even as the 5629 was being cut up, volunteers were working to restore Nickel Plate USRA Light Mikado 587 in Indianapolis. By the fall of 1988 it was running on the Indiana Rail Road's ex-Illinois Central line between Indianapolis and Bloomington, Indiana. *(Mike Schafer)*

Nickel Plate 587 is a USRA original Light Mikado built on government order from Baldwin in 1918 and assigned to the Lake Erie & Western as the 5541 and used on the line to Peoria, Illinois. The LE&W was merged into the Nickel Plate in 1924, and the engine became NKP 587. When the 587 was retired in 1955, its good tender was swapped with the larger tank off sister 639 which had a damaged stoker. Ironically, both engines were preserved, and the 639 resides today in a park in Bloomington, Illinois, with the 587's tender! The "Friends of 587" were delighted to have the bigger tender when they overhauled the 587, as it would give their engine greater range in the modern era of no water or coaling facilities. On September 10, 1988, the 587 made a break-in run by taking a loaded coal train to an Indianapolis power plant on the Indiana Rail Road. The 587 operates today at the Indiana Transportation Museum in Noblesville. *(Steve Brown)*

Burlington's Most-Famous Mike

Like a character actor in a movie, fame is not always a function of good looks. Such was definitely the case with Chicago, Burlington & Quincy's long-lived 2-8-2 4960. While rail historians agree that the USRA locomotives set a high standard of appearance, not all locomotives of that era could be so generously described. When Baldwin rolled CB&Q 4960 out in July 1923, there was definitely no beauty contest. One of 147 CB&Q Class O1a 2-8-2s, the 4960 was based on a very successful design that dated from 1910. About the same general size as the USRA Light Mikado, the Burlington O1a's were slightly larger and heavier, but with their high-mounted headlights, too-tall cabs, oddly-crowded

The Grand Canyon Railway acquired the 4960 in 1989 and gave it a modern, high-tech overhaul to make it reliable for daily service on the rugged line from Williams, Arizona, to the Grand Canyon. Converted to burn oil and fitted with a tender off a Cotton Belt 4-8-4, the renewed 4960 poses near Williams Junction on October 3, 1997. *(Mike Del Vecchio)*

Hodges trailing trucks and boxy tenders, they had the appearance of a much older design.

But out on the road the O1a's were impressive. With 63-inch drivers, they were able to able to bat along all day at 60 MPH or get down and lug it out with tonnage on a steep grade. They were the type of simple, rugged locomotives that were characteristically American—you could beat 'em up and then fix 'em up, and they'd just keep on running.

When the CB&Q began retiring steam, the 4960 made her debut as an excursion engine on December 28, 1958. For the next six years it was a mainstay on the Burlington's system-wide excursion program. Good for 65 MPH on the main lines, the 4960 was usually used at more moderate speeds on branch lines. In the end, it was the 4960 on one of those branchline rambles to an obscure junction called Denrock in northwestern Illinois that wrapped up the CB&Q's steam program on July 17, 1966.

In 1965 and 1966, the 4960 had been loaned out to power an annual historic circus train over the Chicago & North Western to Milwaukee from the Circus World Museum in Baraboo, Wisconsin. As a result, upon retirement the 4960 was donated to the circus museum and soon wound up at the nearby Mid-Continent Railway Museum. After years of dead storage, the 4960 was leased in 1980 to the Bristol & Northwestern tourist railroad in Virginia, where it operated for two seasons before being

(Left) Southern Pacific bought 15 medium 4-6-2s in 1921 for the Overland Route, and three of them were preserved in the Bay Area. The first to be restored was the 2472, by the Golden Gate Railroad Museum, and it made its debut at the Sacramento Railfair in May 1991.

(Below) In a similar scenario, SP 2467 was restored by the Pacific Locomotive Association in Oakland just in time for Railfair 1999. En route to Sacramento, it paused at Fairfield/Suisun on June 16, 1999.

retired again when the B&NW's owner, Harold Keene, became too ill to manage his railroad.

In 1989 the 4960 was sold to the newly-created Grand Canyon Railway in Arizona, to embark upon an entirely new career. She was given a high-tech overhaul and converted to burn oil for the 64-mile run from Williams, Arizona, to the rim of the Grand Canyon. The railroad gave the 4960 a new tender and "USRA style" headlight and front-end treatment, but underneath you can still see the old Burlington hog.

The 4960 may not be pretty, but a good character actor can always find work.

Southern Pacific Pacifics

The two USRA designs pretty well defined the basic parameters of the 4-6-2 for all time. That's not to say, however, that no other Pacifics were built during that era. In January 1921, the Southern Pacific was taking delivery from Baldwin of 15 Class P8 4-6-2s (Nos. 2460–2474) for use between Ogden,

Utah, and Sparks (Reno), Nevada, primarily hauling the *Overland Limited*. This was a 536-mile run, which the Pacifics would make every day with an 11-car heavyweight train. The P8s were seven tons heavier than a USRA Light Pacific with the same 73-inch drivers, and they were just slightly smaller overall than the Pennsylvania K4s. The SP P8s could sprint across the Great Salt Lake on the Lucin Cutoff and then tackle the 1½ percent grades in the Nevada foothills without helper engines.

When larger locomotives bumped them off the Overland Route, the P8s were transferred to commute service between San Francisco and San Jose,

In the 1920s the Atlanta & West Point and Western Railway of Alabama teamed up to handle the Southern Railway's *Crescent Limited* between Atlanta, Georgia, and Montgomery, Alabama. Here at Atlanta's Terminal Station on August 16, 1946, A&WP's Lima 4-6-2 290 has arrived at 1:25 PM with No. 38, the eastbound *Crescent Limited*. (Raymond B. Carneal, James G. Bogle collection)

where they hauled rush-hour passengers until the end of steam. Three of these fine locomotives were saved from the scrappers and displayed at various places in the Bay Area. In the 1980s two different groups of volunteers went to work on two of the preserved P8s, and the first to complete the job was the Project 2472 from the Golden Gate Railroad Museum. In May 1991, SP 2472 was the surprise "star" of Railfair 1991, celebrating the tenth anniversary of the California State Railroad Museum in Sacramento. In a nearly identical scenario eight years later, the Project 2467 group from the Pacific Locomotive Association in Oakland had sister 2467 ready just in time for California's Sesquicentennial Railfair in June 1999.

The West Point Limas

Back in 1926, the Atlanta & West Point and Western Railway of Alabama were handling the Southern Railway's *Crescent Limited* over their "West Point Route" between Atlanta, Georgia, and Montgomery, Alabama. The task required one locomotive in each direction per day, so the schedule could be covered by two locomotives. Since the Southern would bring the train from Washington, D.C., into Atlanta behind one of its famous green-and-gold Ps4 heavy Pacifics, the West Point Route had two nearly identical engines built by the Lima Locomotive Works. The WofA 190 and A&WP 290 differed from a Ps4 only in minor details, such as having a modern cast-steel trailing truck, but their perfor-

mance specifications were identical to the Ps4.

The 190 and 290 were the undisputed queens of the West Point Route, and when diesels arrived in 1954, the 190 was scrapped, but the 290 was presented to the City of Atlanta in 1958 for display in Lakewood Park. When Graham Claytor was expanding his Southern Railway steam program in the 1970s, he made numerous offers to acquire the 290 to make her into an ersatz Southern Ps4 in green and gold. The fiercely independent West Point Route was willing to go along with one excep-tion: "The locomotive must remain painted A&WP 290." Thus, the closest Mr. Claytor came to a Ps4 was his green Mikado 4501.

But the story doesn't end there. The Atlanta Chapter of the National Railway Historical Society acquired the 290 and began a restoration for use on the New Georgia Railroad, which was operating tourist trains on CSX trackage throughout the city. When she steamed again in 1989, it was as A&WP 290, not a Southern Ps4. The West Point Route had stood its ground and won the game.

Looking unchanged from its 1946 image (opposite), Atlanta & West Point 290 rolled across the old Seaboard Air Line's South Peachtree Creek viaduct in Atlanta on May 3, 1992, with a New Georgia Railroad chartered excursion over CSX lines around the city.

(Above) The Frisco had a reputation for well-maintained locomotives. The 4113 was one of 65 copies of the USRA Heavy Mikado built in the mid-1920s with Delta trailing trucks. The 4113 was recorded at St. Louis on August 11, 1948, and the photo notes: "25 days, 7,350 miles without dropping fires." *(H. L. Wilson, Railfan & Railroad collection)*

(Below) On behalf of the Burlington Northern, which absorbed the St. Louis-San Francisco in 1980, Frisco 4-8-2 1522 made several guest appearances at events like the annual Galesburg (Illinois) Railroad Days, where it is on display in June 1995. *(Mike Schafer)*

The Ozark Mountain

The 4-8-2 was the logical outgrowth of the 4-6-2. Alco built the first in 1911 with a batch of 4-8-2s for the Chesapeake & Ohio which were to be used on the Mountain Division between Charlottesville and Clifton Forge, Virginia—hence the name "Mountain" type. Seven years later the USRA hit near perfection with its two 4-8-2 designs.

Typically built with drivers ranging from 69 to 73 inches, the 4-8-2s were heavy passenger and fast freight engines. The 4-8-2 design arrived just in time to handle the much heavier passenger trains that resulted when wooden cars were replaced by stronger and safer all-steel passenger cars, known as "heavyweights."

In the 1920s the St. Louis-San Francisco Railway, better known as the "Frisco," had a tradition of handsome Georgian styling on its clean and well-maintained locomotives—passenger engines were adorned with pinstripes like fine French Louis XVI furniture. Among the most highly regarded of all the Frisco engines were the 30 1500-class 4-8-2s built by Baldwin between 1923 and 1926.

One of these was the 1522, which spent most of its career hauling heavyweight passenger trains between Kansas City, Memphis, Birmingham, Oklahoma City, and St. Louis. Built as a coal burner, the 1522 was soon converted to oil. Her 69½-inch drivers and overall size made her quick to accelerate and capable of making time on the Frisco's curves and hills. When diesels took over the passenger assignments, the 1522 went into freight service, where she wrapped up a long career in 1951 by working local freight out of Fort Smith, Arkansas.

The 1522 was proudly donated to the National Museum of Transport in St. Louis and in 1985 was leased to the St. Louis Steam Train Association for restoration and excursion use. After three years of hard work, the 1522 rolled out under steam and was one of the loudest and lustiest steam locomotives that had been heard on American railroads in years. Another "basic Baldwin" at heart, the 1522 even sounds like the 1920s. She is the pure embodiment of that golden age of American railroading known as "the Standard Era."

Frisco 4-8-2 1522 was romping at track speed westward through Moselle, Missouri, on home track on June 16, 1990, with a trip from St. Louis to Newburg for the NRHS Convention. The classic 1926 Baldwin was making some impressive exhaust sound, accented by its deep-toned whistle.

Two of the West's finest 4-8-4s journeyed to Los Angeles to help celebrate the 50th Anniversary of the magnificent Los Angeles Union Passenger Terminal. On May 6, 1989, Southern Pacific "Daylight" 4-8-4 4449 (built by Lima in 1941) steams alongside Union Pacific's gray 4-8-4 8444 (built by Alco in 1943 as the 844) at LAUPT. The SP 4449 had come in from its home in Portland, Oregon, and the 8444 had come across the mountains from Cheyenne, Wyoming.

Super 4 Power

Back in the 1880s, it was the moving of the firebox from between the drivers and placing it above a two-wheel trailing truck that made possible the growth of the steam locomotive into the 4-8-2 and 2-10-2 and even 2-8-8-2 that powered the nation through World War I. A bigger firebox obviously made possible a better boiler and a bigger locomotive. After some calculations and an experimental New York Central 2-8-2 in 1922, Lima's Will Woodard concluded that enlarging the firebox without enlarging the overall boiler would make an even more efficient and powerful locomotive. Instead of going just for pulling power, Woodard decided to emphasize "horsepower," which would deliver that pulling power at a higher speed.

To prove his theory, in February 1925 Lima Locomotive Works turned out a "demonstrator" locomotive of a brand-new wheel arrangement: the 2-8-4. This Lima "A-1" had the 63-inch drivers of a large Mikado, big cylinders, and the biggest firebox placed on any steam locomotive up to that time. To carry the firebox was the first four-wheel trailer truck. The hulking locomotive also had a two-cylinder booster engine on the trailing truck to aid in starting a heavy train (this gear-driven booster cut out at speeds over 10 MPH). This 2-8-4 was tested with spectacular success in the Berkshire Mountains of New England on the Boston & Albany Railroad, and the 2-8-4 type was known thereafter as the "Berkshire." Every locomotive built with a four-wheel trailer truck can trace its basic engineering back to Lima's A-1.

Following the success of the A-1 2-8-4, Lima stretched out the design with one more set of drivers to create the first 2-10-4 for the Texas & Pacific (hence the type name "Texas"). Ten T&P 2-10-4s were delivered the same year that the A-1 was

No other locomotive better represented the idea of "Super Power" than the Nickel Plate Road's 80 handsome Berkshires. Designed for fast freight, these 69-inch-drivered 2-8-4s were the perfect locomotives for the flat terrain between Buffalo and Chicago and St. Louis. The first Nickel Plate "Berk" to be restored after the end of steam was the 759, which was overhauled by Ross Rowland's High Iron Company in the NKP roundhouse at Conneaut, Ohio, where it simmered under steam on September 7, 1968, the night before its first run following restoration. *(Mike Schafer)*

(Right) In the early 1920s, Lima design engineer Will Woodard theorized that a larger firebox would result in more power at speed. He tried out his "Super Power" idea on a heavy Mikado that became the New York Central's H10 class. NYC H10b 2374 and a sister are westbound at Ann Arbor, Michigan in July 1948. *(Elmer Treloar, Railfan & Railroad collection)*

(Below) Woodard enlarged his "big Mike" with a much bigger firebox carried on a four-wheel trailer truck that resulted in the first 2-8-4, a prototype Lima called the A-1. Illinois Central purchased the A-1 which became IC 8049, shown at Bluford, Illinois, on July 11, 1948. *(R. J. Foster, Railfan & Railroad collection)*

introduced (1925). The T&P ultimately acquired 70 of those 2-10-4s.

The first locomotive of the T&P's second order, the 610, was built by Lima in June 1927. After a long career in heavy freight service, T&P 610 was donated for display at Fort Worth in 1951. In 1975 she was chosen by proud Texans to head up the *American Freedom Train* through her home state, and a complete overhaul was funded. Following her *Freedom Train* tour, the 610 was leased to the

Southern Railway from February 1977 to January 1981 and operated in excursion service throughout the Southeast and Appalachia. After returning to Texas, in 1987, the 610 was put on display on the Texas State Railroad at Palestine.

Although the 610 had been rebuilt by the T&P in 1938 with improved drivers and lightweight rods, the 610's operations on the Southern illustrated the one drawback of the early Super Power design: the 63-inch drivers and heavy rods. As built, the 610

The Texas & Pacific 2-10-4s were the Lima A-1 2-8-4 stretched out with one more set of drivers. T&P 610, at Cincinnati, Ohio, on July 17, 1977, clearly shows the "Lima Articulated Back End" four-wheel truck also used on the A-1. This is actually the rear of the underframe, and the locomotive pulls the tender and train through the truck.

73

That big horizontal tank across the front of Texas & Pacific 2-10-4 610 is an Elesco feedwater heater that uses exhaust steam to pre-heat the water that is pumped into the boiler. The Lima A-1 2-8-4, the Boston & Albany "Berkshires" that were duplicates of it, and the T&P 2-10-4s all had this distinctive "face." After the Illinois Central bought the A-1 demonstrator and its initial order of Berks, it removed the feedwater heaters, feeling that they did not improve efficiency enough to justify the expense of maintenance, as shown on IC 8049 on page 72. When the Southern Railway leased the 610 for its excursion program in 1977, it retained the T&P "look," including the brass red diamond plate on the feedwater heater, but added such characteristic Southern details as the heralds on the air pump shields and a brass eagle over the headlight—but at least it didn't get painted green! On September 3, 1977, the 610 was double-headed with the green Mikado 4501 to assault Norfolk & Western's infamous Blue Ridge Grade east of Roanoke with a passenger train for the NRHS National Convention.

was a 45-MPH machine, though as rebuilt she was good for about 55. While the A-1 could out-perform 63-inch-drivered Mikados, Lima quickly discovered that they were limiting their boiler and firebox performance with an overly-conservative running gear.

Van Sweringen Berkshires

Although the Texas type had been created by enlarging a Berkshire, the ultimate perfection of the 2-8-4 would come from scaling-down a 2-10-4! In the 1920s the two Van Sweringen brothers from Cleveland were putting together a Northeastern railroad empire that included the Erie, Nickel Plate, and Chesapeake & Ohio systems. Their first task was to "rescue" the ailing Erie, and a new locomotive was to be their tool. Impressed by the performance of the Lima A-1, Erie management worked with Lima to produce an improved Berkshire. Their answer was a slightly bigger boiler than the A-1 atop 70-inch drivers, and the new locomotive was an impressive performer.

During development of the Erie 2-8-4, the Van Sweringens assembled a team known as the Advisory Mechanical Committee to design locomotives for all of their railroads. With an eye toward replacing the powerful but slow 2-8-8-2s on C&O coal trains, the AMC worked with Lima to create the largest two-cylinder locomotive to date, an awesome 2-10-4. The C&O T1 of 1930 improved upon the Erie 2-8-4s with slight adjustments in driver size and cylinder dimensions, giving the new locomotive more tractive power without adversely affecting its speed. A bigger boiler with a combus-

The Van Sweringen brothers of Cleveland were the owners of several big railroads in 1927, including the ailing Erie. Their mechanical committee worked with locomotive builders Alco and Lima to improve upon the prototype A-1 2-8-4 by increasing the driver size from 63 to 70 inches for greater speed. The results were impressive. Erie 3364, built by Baldwin in 1928, is shown at Secaucus, New Jersey, in June 1939. Note that it retains the distinctive Lima trailing truck. *(Robert F. Collins)*

(Above) Van Sweringen's Advisory Mechanical Committee found the perfect proportions for a high-speed freight locomotive in 1930 when they designed Chesapeake & Ohio's T1-class 2-10-4s with 69-inch drivers. Here the powerful and handsome 3032 brings lake coal through Fostoria, Ohio, in August 1949. *(J. J. Young Jr.)*

(Right) When the Pennsylvania Railroad needed a proven heavy freight locomotive at the onset of World War II, it borrowed the design of the C&O T1's and added its own distinctive details, such as the high-set headlight and rounded cab windows. PRR 6456 was photographed in the mid-1950s at Bellevue, Ohio. *(Martin Zak)*

76

tion chamber and higher pressure gave the 2-10-4 greater steaming capacity and horsepower. The 40 C&O T1s were not only an unqualified success on their home road, but at the onset of World War II the Pennsylvania Railroad chose the T1 as a basis for 125 of its own 2-10-4s—the J1 class—which are often regarded as the best locomotives the PRR ever owned.

The AMC applied the lessons of the C&O T1 to a new 2-8-4 for the flat and fast Nickel Plate, creating what was essentially "70 percent of a T1" in size and power but which retained 100 percent of its efficiency. The resulting Nickel Plate Berkshire became one of the most successful locomotive designs in history—they were perfectly matched to the Nickel Plate's speed and tonnage requirements and proved to be legendary performers, with a total of 80 being built between 1934 and 1949. Because the "Berks" performed so well in the fast freight service for which the Nickel Plate was

Although the Advisory Mechanical Committee worked with Lima to develop the Nickel Plate 2-8-4 by downscaling the C&O 2-10-4, it was Alco that won the bid for NKP's first 15 700s in 1934. "Class engine" 700 is storming upgrade on Peoria-bound train 65 at Summit (Purdue Airport), Indiana, in 1951. (Hal Lewis)

77

On the morning of September 8, 1968, Nickel Plate Berkshire 759 eased out of the Conneaut, Ohio, roundhouse and backed onto its passenger train in the adjacent freight yard, preparing for its first excursion run to Buffalo and back. Berkshires like the 759 had been handling fast freight between Bellevue and Buffalo until early summer 1958.

rightly famous, it was one of the last to dieselize and continued to dispatch 2-8-4s on tonnage until the middle of 1958.

There were six Nickel Plate Berks preserved, and the first to be returned to service was 759, which was leased from the Steamtown U.S.A. collection by Ross Rowland's High Iron Company of New Jersey. It was overhauled in the Nickel Plate roundhouse in Conneaut, Ohio, and made a debut on a run to Buffalo on September 8, 1968. For the next four years the 759 operated numerous trips in the Northeast in addition to the *Golden Spike Centennial Limited* in May 1969 from New York to Kansas

City. In 1972 the 759 was returned to Steamtown and is now at Scranton, Pennsylvania.

In 1963 the 765 had been donated to the City of Fort Wayne, Indiana, and placed in a city park. She was retrieved in 1974 by the Fort Wayne Railroad Historical Society and returned to steam in 1979. Over the next 15 years the 765 handled passenger excursions all over the Midwest and Northeast.

With the success of the first Nickel Plate 2-8-4s in 1934, the Van Sweringens went on to develop nearly identical locomotives for the Pere Marquette; the Wheeling & Lake Erie; the Chesapeake & Ohio; the Richmond, Fredericksburg & Potomac;

Decked out with blue and gold trim for the *Golden Spike Centennial Limited*, the 759 steams out of Lima, Ohio, in May 1969 on its return trip from Kansas City to New York, celebrating the centennial of the completion of the first transcontinental railroad on May 10, 1869. In the background is the Lima Locomotive Works, where Nickel Plate 759 had been built in August 1944.

The second Nickel Plate Berkshire to be resurrected was the 765, which had been on display in a park in Fort Wayne, Indiana. The Fort Wayne Railroad Historical Society overhauled the 765 in the late 1970s and had it back under steam by 1979. In May 1980 the 765 spent a week on the Toledo, Peoria & Western in central Illinois in freight and excursion passenger service. On Tuesday night, May 6, the 759 stops for water at Gilman, Illinois, while working regularly scheduled local freight No. 24 from East Peoria to Watseka (departing with seven loads and 30 empties, 1,439 tons). That's the Illinois Central depot in the background. Aboard the 759 was TP&W President Bob McMillan, who had been a fireman on IC steam.

(Facing page) On another day during the same week of TP&W service, the 765 and its freight payload made for an unlikely encounter along U.S. Highway 24—motorists probably hadn't seen steam on this line for a quarter century. *(Mike Schafer)*

The ten 2-8-4s built by Lima for the Richmond, Fredericksburg & Potomac in 1943 differed from Nickel Plate 2-8-4s only in minor details such as dome placement. RF&P 572 is shown at Richmond, Virginia, in March 1949. *(A. A. Theime, Charles T. Felstead collection)*

and the Virginian Railway. By the time production ended with Nickel Plate 779 in 1949 (the last steam locomotive built by Lima), 257 2-8-4s had been built for six different railroads to the basic Van Sweringen design.

Northerns and Hudsons

In the mid-1920s the Northern Pacific was looking for a locomotive that could eliminate doubleheading on passenger trains in the mountains and could burn the low-grade "Rosebud" coal mined

Chesapeake & Ohio "Kanawhas" looked quite different from Nickel Plate Berkshires. C&O 2713 was at Handley, West Virginia, in 1951. *(Paul Gorath, Railfan & Railroad collection)*

When George Brook left the presidency of the C&O in 1937 to become chairman of the neighboring Virginian Railway, he adopted C&O designs for new Virginian locomotives, including five 2-8-4s built by Lima in 1946 based on identical C&O 2700-series engines. The 505 is at Roanoke, Virginia, in 1947. *(L. M. Kelly, Herbert H. Harwood collection)*

Between 1934 and 1944, the Pere Marquette bought 39 2-8-4s based on the Nickel Plate design. PM 1225 ran at the National Railway Historical Society convention in Huntington, West Virginia, in August 1991 (see also page 2).

Wheeling & Lake Erie had 31 Berkshires built by Alco between 1937 and 1942 based on the Nickel Plate design but equipped with inboard-bearing pilot trucks and boxpok drivers. Wheeling 6403 is rolling 139 loads of coal through Warrenton, Ohio, as the engineer prepares to grab the train-order hoop from station operator Charlie Fisher. *(J. J. Young Jr.)*

in Montana. Working with Alco, NP developed a 4-8-2 with a much bigger firebox for the native coal and replaced the two-wheel trailing truck with a four-wheeled truck, resulting in a 4-8-4. In 1926 and 1927 the NP took delivery of the first twelve 4-8-4s (2600–2611), which gave the "Northern" type its name. These engines had 73-inch driving wheels, which yielded a good balance between power and speed.

At that time the Atchison, Topeka & Santa Fe was facing a similar problem in powering the *Chief*, a new heavyweight passenger train on a fast schedule between Chicago and Los Angeles. Baldwin built a single 4-8-4 for evaluation purposes. The wheel arrangement was so new that the engine was called simply a "heavy Mountain" instead of a "Northern."

Santa Fe 4-8-4 3751 rolled out in May 1927 on 69-inch driving wheels, which gave it more pulling power than the 4-8-2s it replaced. In a comparison

The seven 2-8-4s built for the Pittsburgh & Lake Erie by Alco in 1948 were definitely not a Van Sweringen design. In spite of their massive appearance, these engines had only 63-inch driving wheels, which made them much slower machines—which would be no problem on the shorter and much more congested P&LE. The 9400–9406 were the last steam locomotives built by Alco for a U.S. railroad. *(G. C. Corey, Ed Crist collection)*

The "Big Three" Builders

BY THE MID-1920s, there were three major commercial locomotive builders in the United States. The oldest and largest was the Baldwin Locomotive Works, founded by Matthias Baldwin in Philadelphia in 1831. In 1926 Baldwin opened its new Eddystone Works on the south side of town, which had 108 acres under roof. Baldwin was one of the first builders to standardize components and production techniques, and its locomotives could best be described as basic locomotives of straightforward design and rugged construction.

In 1901, the Schenectady Locomotive Works of upstate New York merged with seven other smaller regional companies to create the American Locomotive Company, known simply as Alco. By 1928 the outlying plants had been closed down, and all production was carried on at Schenectady. While Baldwin built the workaday locomotives, Alco built the aristocrats in the form of sleek passenger engines, three-cylinder freight engines and ultimately the world's largest articulateds.

In 1880 Ephraim Shay invented a strange-looking little gear-driven contraption to haul logs on temporary track and built the first one at the Lima Machine Works in its namesake city in western Ohio. The "Shay"-type locomotive was an immediate success, and over the next 65 years 2,800 of his geared locomotives were produced at Lima. In 1901 the company became the Lima Locomotive Works and added conventional rod-driven locomotives to its production. Under the engineering leadership of Will Woodard, Lima became the most serious innovator of the Big Three, taking the basic physics of steam and combustion and developing the design

The smallest of the "Big Three" steam locomotive builders was the Lima Locomotive Works of Lima, Ohio. In January 1944 the brand new Nickel Plate 2-8-4 740 was ready for delivery to the customer, whose roundhouse was adjacent to the Lima factory. *(Railfan & Railroad collection)*

elements that would carry steam locomotives into the modern realm it termed "Super Power." Additionally, Lima was known for its unparalleled craftsmanship and well-engineered design.

Although each of the builders became known for locomotives that reflected their individual design philosophies, they were also capable of turning out the typical mass-production locomotives that did most of the work and made few headlines. Regardless of builder, American locomotives tended to be big, simple, robust and rugged. They were built for power and ease of maintenance compared to the complex but efficient and smaller power found elsewhere in the world.

Although not a locomotive builder as such, one other company should be included in the same mention as the Big Three. In 1925 the General Steel Castings Corporation of Granite City, Illinois, introduced the Commonwealth Cast Locomotive Bed, which made possible the large, modern locomotives of the next quarter century. In one huge steel casting, GSC could deliver to the locomotive builder (the Big Three or any railroad shop) a rigid, one-piece locomotive frame that included the cast-in cylinders, mounting pads for valve gear and crossheads, and often even internal air reservoirs. These castings eliminated the often troublesome bolts and welds that held together the frames and cylinders on older locomotives. In addition to cast engine beds, GSC also produced the large castings for the modern Delta-style trailing trucks. In short, General Steel Castings made possible many of the locomotives that the designers were dreaming up.

test, the 4-8-4 developed 3,220 drawbar horse-power at 40 MPH, while the 4-8-2 hit only 2,380, and the 4-8-4 did it on 38.7 percent less coal. Satisfied, the Santa Fe immediately acquired 13 more, and the new engines, Nos. 3752–3764, went to work in Arizona and New Mexico along with the 3751.

By 1930 the 4-8-4 had proven itself to be the universal "big engine," capable of fast passenger service and heavy freight work—for the first time since the 4-4-0, America had a true "dual service" locomotive again. It was heavy enough to get the optimum traction from eight drivers while being powerful enough in the boiler to permit larger drivers for greater speed. While 2-8-4s and 4-8-2s used drivers from 63 to 73 inches, the 4-8-4s went from 69 to 80 inches, delivering both greater power and speed.

The 4-8-4 was also the first wheel arrangement to test the full potential of roller bearings on all axles, a concept introduced on Timken Roller Bearing Company's demonstrator 1111, built by Alco in 1930 and ultimately sold to the Northern Pacific as 2626. The Timken "Four Aces" 4-8-4 proved its point, and from the mid-1930s on, most new locomotives were equipped with roller bearings.

The Hudson Emerges

While the four-wheel trailer truck and the philosophy of horsepower design was first applied to freight locomotives like the 2-8-4, it didn't take long to turn the tried-and-true passenger 4-6-2 into a Super Power 4-6-4. In 1925, the same year that Lima turned out its A1 2-8-4, Milwaukee Road motive power chief C. H. Bilty was working with Baldwin on the design of a 4-6-4 passenger engine with 79-inch drivers. The railroad went bankrupt before it could be built, however, and the first 4-6-4 "Milwaukee" type would be upstaged by the New York

The first 4-8-4 was created in 1926 when Alco put an oversized firebox on what was essentially a 4-8-2 so it could burn low-grade coal mined along the Northern Pacific. The 2604 was one of those twelve pioneer 4-8-4s built for the NP. It is shown on a troop train running as the first section of the eastbound *North Coast Limited* out of Spokane in 1950. *(Philip R. Hastings, Railfan & Railroad collection)*

(Below right) The first steam locomotive to have roller bearings on all axles was the Timken Roller Bearing Company's demonstrator 4-8-4 No. 1111, built by Alco in 1930. After testing on 14 different railroads and proving the value of roller bearings, the "Four Aces" was sold to the Northern Pacific. *(Timken)*

(Below) Northern Pacific 2626 was the former Timken 1111, which the railroad purchased in 1933. Throughout its career the 2626 carried a reference to Timken on its tender. In spite of the NP's willingness to cooperate, efforts to save this historic locomotive failed, and it was scrapped in 1958. *(Northern Pacific)*

Central's Paul W. Keifer, who also calculated that simply enlarging the firebox over a four-wheel trailer truck would produce a locomotive of roughly one-third more capacity than a Pacific of similar size. As a result, it was Alco that first put Keifer's theory to work on February 14, 1927, with a single 4-6-4 for the New York Central—and gave the wheel arrangement the name "Hudson," after New York State's most famous river.

With NYC J1a-class 5200, Alco and Keifer had created a classic. Seldom has the first version of a new wheel arrangement produced such an unqual-ified success. Even through the design was refined over the years as 275 were built, the 79-inch drivers, basic dimensions and unusually clean lines of the original 5200 were clearly evident. Easily capable of 90-MPH speeds, the Hudsons became world famous. A few were even given stylish streamlined shrouds for handling such premier trains as the *20th Century Limited* and the *Empire State Express.* And railroaders will forever compare the NYC's modern Hudsons to the rival Pennsylvania Rail-road's "archaic" K4s Pacifics. Unfortunately, the dis-cussion will never get beyond theory, for although

two examples of the K4s survive, not a single NYC Hudson was saved—one of the great tragedies of steam locomotive preservation history.

After the impressive performance of the New York Central's J1a in 1927, the 4-6-4 became the obvious successor to the 4-6-2 for fast passenger service. It wasn't long before 4-6-4s could be found running nearly everywhere, from the little Maine Central to monsters on the Santa Fe, Chicago & North Western, and Milwaukee Road with 84-inch drivers and 300-psi boiler pressure.

Burlington 4-6-4s and 4-8-4s

In 1930 the Chicago, Burlington & Quincy was seeking bigger power for both freight and passenger service, and that year Baldwin began building eight new 4-8-4s and twelve 4-6-4s side-by-side at Eddystone for the "Q." They shared many common design elements and looked quite similar, although the Hudsons had 78-inch drivers and the 4-8-4s had 74s. Both designs were very successful, and the Burlington wanted many more of the 4-8-4s—which Burlington classed as O5's—for freight.

Burlington's method for acquiring new 4-8-4s was typical of many railroads that had good back-shops. Wishing to keep employment "at home" during the Depression, in 1936 the CB&Q began building the new 4-8-4s at its shop in West Burlington, Iowa. "Assembled" would probably be a more proper word, for the West Burlington O5's consisted of boilers built by Baldwin being mated to General Steel Castings engine beds and equipped

Paul W. Keifer worked closely with Alco to design the first 4-6-4 in 1927 for the New York Central, and the locomotive was an instant classic. Although its basic dimensions remained unchanged, the boiler was dramatically improved over the years, resulting in the "Super Hudson" like J3a 5409, shown here striding along its namesake river at Garrison, New York, with a milk train on April 13, 1938. *(R. P. Morris, Railfan & Railroad collection)*

In one of the finest examples of American industrial design, Henry Dreyfuss styled a streamlined shroud for J3a super Hudsons 5445–5454, which were built new by Alco in March 1938 for the newly streamlined *20th Century Limited*. The roller bearing rods and Scullin disk drivers only enhanced the futuristic look of these magnificent gray machines. Unlike other early attempts at streamlining, Dreyfuss made no attempt to hide the intrinsic shape and compelling machinery of the locomotive. (*New York Central, Railfan & Railroad collection*)

(Right) Milwaukee Road's C. H. Bilty had been working with Baldwin in 1925 on the design of a high-speed 4-6-4, but the railroad went bankrupt before it could be built, and two years later New York Central and Alco got the glory for the first 4-6-4. Bilty's locomotive was finally built in 1929–30 as the 6400–6413. On July 20, 1934, the 80-inch-drivered 6402 proved that a high speed schedule between Chicago and Milwaukee was possible when it hit 103.5 MPH on a test run, shown here upon arrival in Milwaukee. (*H.W. Pontin, Railfan & Railroad collection*)

with Baldwin disc drivers. Air pumps, feedwater heaters, power reverse, and valve gear were all catalog components, purchased and bolted on. Of course, the Big Three commercial builders often purchased these same components themselves and assembled them the same way.

One of the Class O5a 4-8-4s built at West Burlington in 1940 was the 5632, a handsome coal-burner that represented the final refinement of the CB&Q design. She was soon converted to burn oil for use on the lines west of Lincoln, Nebraska, and reclassed O5b. It was the convenience of her oil fuel that resulted in the 5632 being withdrawn from retirement in November 1958 to begin a seven-year career as CB&Q's premier excursion locomotive along with Mikado 4960 (pages 62–65).

(Above) The Chicago, Burlington & Quincy had Baldwin build twelve 4-6-4s and eight 4-8-4s at the same time in 1930, and both designs shared many common elements. Hudson 4000 was rebuilt from the 3002 in 1937 and is now on permanent display at La Crosse, Wisconsin.

(Left) After the initial eight Class O5 4-8-4s were built by Baldwin in 1930, the Chicago, Burlington & Quincy constructed 28 more in its West Burlington shop. The oil-burning O5b 5632, built in 1940, is at Galesburg, Illinois, on May 17, 1964, with an excursion train as the caboose of freight CD61 passed by.

(Left) Weighing in at 395,920 pounds, CB&Q Hudsons were considerably heavier and more powerful than the New York Central's 343,000-pound J1a's. Baldwin made this builder's portrait of the 3000 in 1930. *(H. L. Broadbelt collection)*

This is what a Burlington O5 was all about! On November 24, 1956, the West Burlington-built O5a 5634 was romping westward between Galva and Galesburg, Illinois, at nearly 60 MPH with a 90-car freight train as the photographer raced alongside in a '55 Ford on U.S. 34. Note how the hot steam is nearly invisible immediately above the stack but quickly blossoms into a magnificent white plume as it hits the brisk autumn air. The O5's were famous for their very loud exhaust, and at this speed the 5634 would have sounded like a jet bomber at full throttle! *(Jim Shaughnessy)*

Until retired again in 1965, the 5632 clearly demonstrated why the 4-8-4-type locomotive had come to dominate America's railroads since the 1930s. Although never again called upon to haul 125 freight cars to Galesburg at 45 MPH, the 5632 showed how her class had performed in passenger service, striding effortlessly along all day at 85 MPH with a 20-car heavyweight passenger train—and hitting over 100 MPH on more than one occasion. Typical of the Midwestern 4-8-4s with their "medium size" 74-inch drivers, the Burlington O5's were true dual-service engines in both theory and practice.

And the 5632 gained particular fame for being the "loudest" steam locomotive in excursion service. Her thunderous exhaust would shake the

(Above) The 5632 looks like the world's biggest brass model on May 23, 1964, when it was painted gold to celebrate 100 years of Burlington Route commuter service. The train of 21 modern bilevel cars carried 3,304 passengers between Chicago and Aurora, setting a record for the most people ever carried on a single passenger train.

(Left) During its excursion career in the mid-1960s, Burlington 5632 was generally kept in the Clyde Yard roundhouse in Cicero, Illinois, near Chicago. The CB&Q kept many of its steam facilities intact at Chicago and Galesburg to support the company's popular public-relations steam program.

ground when starting a train, and at speed her stack would blur into a jet-like roar. Of all the locomotives preserved before or since, none has had the sheer presence of the 5632. There are those who contend, however, that under the right circumstances the CB&Q's 4-6-4s could be even louder.

The Pride of Pine Bluff

Although the St. Louis Southwestern Railroad, better known as the "Cotton Belt," had been a subsidiary of the Southern Pacific since 1932, it long retained its separate identity with a fierce sense of local pride. That pride was well justified on a railroad with a 70-MPH main line from St. Louis to Texas. Over the years its *Blue Streak Merchandise* has been one of the hottest freight trains in the country. To this day nothing brings out more pride

in Cotton Belt people than the 800-Class oil-burning 4-8-4s that rolled out of the home shop in Pine Bluff, Arkansas.

In 1930 the biggest freight power on the Cotton Belt was a moderate-sized 2-8-0. The 4-8-4 would be a big jump in performance, and the story of the Cotton Belt 800s is very similar to that of the Burlington O5's, as the first ten Cotton Belts were built by Baldwin in 1930 right alongside the Burlington engines. And like the CB&Q,

(Far right) Veteran St. Louis Southwestern engineer T. D. Davis, who had run the railroad's 800-series 4-8-4s in regular service, is at the throttle of the 819 northbound out of Brinkley, Arkansas, on June 12, 1990, making 50 MPH en route to the NRHS convention in St. Louis.

The St. Louis Southwestern Railroad—the "Cotton Belt"—got its first 4-8-4s from Baldwin in 1930. Like the CB&Q would do with its O5 4-8-4s that were being built at the same time, the Cotton Belt built the rest of its 4-8-4s in its home shop with cast underframes from General Steel Castings and boilers supplied by Baldwin. The 819 was the last new Cotton Belt 4-8-4 to leave the Pine Bluff Shops on February 8, 1943. In 1988 the 819 was overhauled by volunteers in that same shop and went into excursion service with a three-day trip from Pine Bluff to Tyler, Texas, and back. On November 6, 1988, the 819 is westbound at Naples, Texas, with that train.

the SSW built the rest of its fleet in the home shop with Baldwin boilers and GSC engine beds. To give adequate speed with optimum pulling power, the Cotton Belt engines were built with 70-inch drivers, making them a true freight engine.

The last Cotton Belt 4-8-4 was the 819, which was put into service at Pine Bluff on February 8, 1943. Its working life was cut short by the arrival of freight diesels and was retired in 1955 to Pine Bluff's Oakland Park. In 1983 the Cotton Belt Rail Historical Society got the 819 returned to the very shop building where she had been built back in 1943. After spending over $140,000 in donated

money and 37,000 man-hours of volunteered time, the 819 steamed on April 17, 1986. The 819 was truly the "Pride of Pine Bluff" again.

The Northwest's Own 4-8-4

Alco built the first dozen 4-8-4s for the Northern Pacific in 1926, but that railroad continued to improve and enlarge on the design. By 1938 the NP was into the third version of its 4-8-4s with eight Class A3s (2660–2667) on order from Baldwin. The NP and neighbor Great Northern had joint control of the Spokane, Portland & Seattle, which carried both roads' traffic down the Columbia River to

On the second day of its debut trip, November 6, 1988, the 819 storms westward past the Pine Grocery store in Pine, Texas. Although impressive in appearance, the Cotton Belt 800s were rather small for 4-8-4s and were actually smaller and less powerful than a Nickel Plate 2-8-4. They were, however, well suited to the railroad's needs and performed well.

Portland, Oregon. The SP&S was in need of modern passenger power, and three locomotives were added to the NP order. The SP&S 700–702 differed from the NP A3s only in being built as oil burners, whereas the NP engines were coal burners. The NP and SP&S engines had 77-inch drivers and full roller bearings, making them exceptional passenger locomotives.

SP&S 700 pulled that railroad's last steam-powered passenger train on May 20, 1956, after which it was donated to the City of Portland, Oregon, for display in Oaks Park. In 1990 the 700 was returned to service by the Pacific Railroad Preservation Association and began a series of outings on the Burlington Northern Railroad. The decades of retirement had done nothing to diminish the capabilities of this impressive example of the "middle" stages of development of the 4-8-4 as a heavy passenger engine.

Milwaukee's "War Babies"

The Chicago, Milwaukee, St. Paul & Pacific—better known as the Milwaukee Road—was an unfortunate victim of history in that its pioneer 4-6-4 design could not be built until after the New York Central had stolen the glory and the name. The first 14 of those Milwaukee 4-6-4s were delivered in 1930, and at that same time Baldwin enlarged the design by one set of drivers to produce a single experimental Milwaukee 4-8-4 (Class S1 No. 9700, later renumbered 250). Like the CB&Q 4-6-4s and 4-8-4s abuilding at Baldwin that same year, the Milwaukee engines shared many design elements and common parts.

Very pleased with its 4-6-4s, the Milwaukee felt no immediate need for more passenger 4-8-4s and waited until 1937 to invest in heavy freight 4-8-4s. The new S2 4-8-4s had the same 74-inch drivers but were heavier and more powerful than the impressive CB&Q O5a's. By 1940 the Milwaukee had 40 freight S2s (201–240) operating out of Chicago to Minneapolis and Omaha. Meanwhile the Milwaukee had acquired four fast 84-inch drivered streamlined 4-4-2s (built 1935–1937) and six super 4-6-4s (built 1938) for its speedy *Hiawatha* passenger trains.

In 1937 the Milwaukee Road was seeking a fast heavy freight locomotive and turned to Baldwin for 30 modern 4-8-4s with roller bearings and 74-inch drivers. The new Milwaukee S2's, Nos. 200–229, were heavier and more powerful than the CB&Q O5 4-8-4s. Ten more were delivered in 1940. The 205 is shown heading west with a freight at Davis Junction, Illinois, in 1947. *(T.V. Maguire, courtesy Milwaukee Road Historical Association)*

(Above) During World War II the Milwaukee needed heavy passenger engines, and Alco delivered "dual service" 4-8-4s 260–269. The 262 posed in 1943 for a builder's photo. *(Alco, courtesy Milwaukee Road Historical Association)*

(Left) Retrieved from the museum in Green Bay and restored by Friends of the 261, the 261 speeds along the old CB&Q west of Galva, Illinois, on June 27, 1998—the same place where CB&Q O5 5634 is shown running on page 90.

95

Milwaukee Road 261 eases up alongside Bridge 60 Tower in the former Delaware, Lackawanna & Western yard now used by the Steamtown National Historic Site in Scranton, Pennsylvania, on the night of February 17, 1996. In its "after life" in the 1990s, the 261 got as far east as Pennsylvania and ranged the West with an "Employee Appreciation Special" for the new (1996) Burlington Northern & Santa Fe system.

With the onset of World War II, the Milwaukee needed more heavy passenger engines, but wartime restrictions prohibited new designs and the building of any pure passenger locomotives. The S2 freight 4-8-4s could not be duplicated, since they were too big to fit into Chicago Union Station on a passenger train. Alco came up with a solution by taking the boiler from a Rock Island 4-8-4 and mating it to the 74-inch drivered running gear of a Delaware & Hudson 4-8-4 and adding a standard Union Pacific tender to create the Milwaukee Road S3 "War Baby" dual-service 4-8-4s. In mid-1944 the Milwaukee took delivery of ten S3s (Nos. 260–269), and they were exactly what the railroad needed.

The S3s were all built as coal burners, but in 1950 four were converted to burn oil and sent to Idaho and Washington for passenger service.

At the end of steam in the late 1950s, only two big Milwaukee Road engines escaped the scrappers: S3s 261 and 265. The 261 went to the National Railroad Museum in Green Bay while the 265 went on display in a Milwaukee park and was later moved to the Illinois Railway Museum. In 1991 Steve Sandberg from Minneapolis leased the 261 from the Green Bay museum, gave it a masterful overhaul, and, on September 18, 1993, launched it on a new career of charters and excursions ranging far and wide.

The Reading Ramblers

The Reading Company (that's RED-ing) had many lines in eastern Pennsylvania, but the longest main line run was less than 200 miles. The railroad had been built to move anthracite coal from the mines around Shamokin to the markets in Harrisburg, Philadelphia and New York City. Reading steam power at the end of World War II was ancient, powerful and slow. Ponderous 2-8-0s and low-drivered Mikados handled most of the road freights.

With the conversion to oil for home heating, the bottom fell out of the anthracite traffic, and the Reading discovered that its new business was handling fast freight from numerous connecting railroads—and its best motive power could hardly maintain 35 MPH without beating up the track. In 1945 the ingenious Dutchmen in the Reading

The Reading created its 4-8-4s by adding a new section to the boilers of heavy but slow 2-8-0s like this I10sa, No. 2018, and putting them on new GSC cast underframes. The 2102 was converted from the 2044 in October 1945. *(Martin S. Zak)*

(Left) The 2102 was one of three Reading 4-8-4s to be used in "Reading Rambles" excursions between 1959 and 1964. It was then sold to a series of private owners and operated as far away as Illinois and West Virginia before returning home. On September 21, 1985, the 2102 steams in front of the Reading Shop where she had been built from a 2-8-0 back in 1945.

Shop came up with a novel way to create a fast freight engine by taking the boilers from their biggest 2-8-0s, lengthening them with one new boiler section, and placing them atop new GSC cast 4-8-4 engine beds.

The resulting T1-class engines had 70-inch drivers and were gutsy performers, able to highball the merchandise at 50 MPH or better speeds. With their big fireboxes they were easy to fire and steamed freely. Between 1945 and 1947 the Reading Shop turned out 30 such conversions (2100–2129) and turned the Reading into a hotly competitive carrier no longer dependent on coal traffic.

The Reading retired its steam engines in 1957 but kept a handful of 4-8-4s in reserve. On October 25, 1959, the 2124 was pulled out and steamed up for the first "Iron Horse Ramble" excursion. Over the next five years the 2100 and 2102 joined the Rambles fleet before the program was reluctantly shut down at the end of 1964 after 51 trips. The 2124 went immediately to the Steamtown U.S.A. collection, and the 2100, 2101, and 2102 were sold to a scrap dealer in Baltimore, who decided to hold the engines and not cut them up.

Aside from a few being leased briefly to the neighboring Pennsylvania Railroad, the Reading

(Left) Following its *Freedom Train* stint *(see below)*, the 2101 was decked out in diesel colors for the *Chessie Steam Special* shown crossing the Susquehanna River at Havre de Grace, Maryland, on April 23, 1977.

(Below) In the spring of 1975 Ross Rowland bought Reading 4-8-4 2101 from the Striegel scrap yard and in just 32 days had it overhauled to handle the Eastern routes of the *American Freedom Train*, which toured the country as a Bicentennial event. It is shown at Lake Hopatcong, New Jersey, in July 1976.

T1's had seldom found themselves more than a half-day's run from the shop in Reading where they'd been built. That took a dramatic change when the 2102 was bought from the scrapper by Bill Benson of Akron, Ohio, and became one of the first privately owned locomotives to operate on a main line far from home. In 1968 she ventured as far west as the Grand Trunk Western in Chicago and embarked on a series of trips over the next few years on the C&O in West Virginia and then back home to the Northeast.

The 2102 returned to Reading in 1985 and was sold to Andy Muller's Blue Mountain & Reading tourist railroad, with 13 miles of 60-MPH track where a 4-8-4 could stretch her legs. In 1991 Andy Muller expanded his rail empire by acquiring 124 miles of former-Reading lines in the anthracite coal region north of Reading, and in April of that year he put the 4-8-4 to work on revenue coal trains. The T1 had truly returned home!

The 2102, however, was not the only Reading T1 to be operated. In 1975 the 2100 and 2101 were sold to Ross Rowland's Steam Locomotive Corporation of America (Rowland was the New York commodities broker who had overhauled Nickel Plate

2-8-4 759 in 1968 and had created the *American Freedom Train* in 1974). Only 32 days after her rusting hulk was pulled from Striegel's junk yard, the red, white, and blue 2101 was coupled to the *American Freedom Train* for its first move out of Washington, D.C., on March 29, 1975.

The 2101 served for two years as *Freedom Train* No. 1, handing off the train to SP 4-8-4 4449 for operation west of Chicago. In the following years, the 2101 was taken under the wing of the Chessie System to barnstorm the old C&O and B&O lines as the *Chessie Steam Special*, wearing an incredible rendition of the Chessie's yellow, blue, and vermilion diesel paint job.

In 1979 Chessie 2102 was severely damaged in a roundhouse fire near Cincinnati. Accepting responsibility, the Chessie traded Rowland Chesapeake & Ohio 4-8-4 No. 614 out of the B&O Museum for the 2101, cosmetically restored as *Freedom Train* No. 1.

This was not the end of the Reading T1's, however. The "parts engine" for the 2101 overhaul, sister 2100, was bought by Richard Kughn, the owner of the Lionel model train company. After overhaul in Hagerstown, Maryland, the 2100 rolled out on March 26, 1989, but Kughn's interest had waned, and the 2100 became the first T1 to leave the country when it was sold to a steam operator in western Canada.

Lima's last 4-8-4

With his Chessie 2101 in the B&O Museum, Ross Rowland began an overhaul of the big C&O 4-8-4. The 614 is of noble heritage. The C&O had acquired five 4-8-4s from Lima

in 1935, and the elegant 74-inch-drivered "Greenbriers" (as the C&O named its Northerns) were heavy passenger engines. C&O 600 was the first 4-8-4 built by Lima. Two more Greenbriers were added in 1942, and even as late as 1948, the C&O—which made its living off of West Virginia's bituminous coal—was still in the market for more steam passenger power. The final five Greenbriers, 610–614, were distinctly C&O and awesomely modern in appearance with their low-mounted headlight and lightweight tandem side rods with roller bearings.

Outshopped in the summer of 1948, the 614 was Lima's last 4-8-4. She went immediately into service over the mountains between Newport News, Virginia, and Hinton, West Virginia. With the arrival of diesels in 1952, the Greenbriers proved to the C&O what other railroads had known about 74-inch-drivered 4-8-4s for decades: they make great fast freight engines. By 1956, she was one of the last steam engines working on the C&O, and after years

In 1949 the 614 had train 41, the Tidewater (Newport News, Virginia) section of Chesapeake & Ohio's Cincinnati-bound *George Washington*, at Main Street Station in Richmond, Virginia. *(Stephen Morill, Chesapeake & Ohio Historical Society)*

of storage, in the early 1970s was donated to the B&O Museum.

The 614 steamed out of the Western Maryland roundhouse in Hagerstown, Maryland, on September 11, 1980, and for the next two years romped the Chessie System as far away as Chicago and Florida with the *Chessie Safety Express*, carrying passengers and promoting the Operation Lifesaver grade crossing safety program. The 614's safety career concluded on November 1, 1981, and she went into storage at Hagerstown.

What happened next is the most incredible story since the end of steam. Ross Rowland had created American Coal Enterprises and was engaged in designing a modern computer-controlled, coal-burning steam locomotive in a response to the energy crisis. The "ACE 3000" would look more like a diesel than a steam engine but would still have driving wheels and lightweight side rods. To "develop a data base" for the ACE 3000 project, Chessie System put the 614 on a month-long trial program hauling coal trains between Huntington and Hinton, West Virginia, on the old C&O main line.

It was January 1985, and the weather reached 20 degrees below zero. The 614 was to run six days a week, and in spite of the weather she never missed a trip, handling trains that ranged from 40 loads eastbound (5,100 tons) to 125 empty hoppers westward. Load sensors and boiler instruments were installed in a car behind the tender. Lineside testing included impact sensors on one segment of

After his Chessie 2101 was severely damaged in a roundhouse fire in 1979, Ross Rowland swapped it to the B&O Museum for C&O "Greenbrier" 614, the last 4-8-4 built by Lima. On the night before her dedication on the *Chessie Safety Express,* the 614 simmers at the old B&O Camden Station in Baltimore on September 12, 1980.

Steam Turbines, Then and Now

(Right) The most successful of all the steam-turbine locomotives was Norfolk & Western's *Jawn Henry* of 1954, which was backing down the Blue Ridge grade in Virginia after pushing a coal train uphill in August 1957. The 2300 carried coal in the bunker ahead of the cab, and its boiler faced backward. Power was applied to the rails through four six-wheel trucks carrying three traction motors each. Chesapeake & Ohio built three similar turbines for a new passenger train in 1947, but *The Chessie* was cancelled, and the turbines were scrapped in 1950. The N&W's *Jawn Henry* lasted until the end of 1957. *(J. J. Young Jr.)*

(Left) Although Pennsylvania Railroad 6200 was the only locomotive of its type ever built, this direct-drive 6-8-6 steam turbine was made world famous by an O-gauge Lionel model. The round housing above the center drivers is the traction turbine. This powerful but short-lived engine is shown Englewood station in Chicago on August 20, 1945. *(Paul Eilenberger, Charles T. Felstead collection)*

World War II produced tremendous strides in steam-turbine technology, primarily in naval applications. In 1945 the Pennsylvania Railroad teamed up with Baldwin and Westinghouse to produce a single 6-8-6 that was powered by a 6900-HP direct-drive steam turbine that was geared to the two center driving wheels. The turbine was economical only at high speed, and its maintenance expense was prohibitively high. The 6200 was retired in 1949 and never duplicated.

The Norfolk & Western tried a different approach in 1949 and spent five years developing a steam-turbine-electric. Where the Pennsy engine had the turbine geared directly to the drive wheels, the N&W had the turbine turning a generator, which supplied electricity to 24 traction motors like a diesel-electric. The traction motors gave the "Jawn Henry" the performance of a 4500-HP four-unit diesel of its time. The locomotive ran well and had incredible power, and the N&W was ready to buy 19 more of them when builder Baldwin-Lima-Hamilton jacked up the price, and the N&W bought diesels instead.

(Below) Artist Hal Kattau rendered the ACE 3000 in 1985, but the computer-controlled coal-fired steam locomotive was never built.

(Above) In the early 1980s steam entrepreneur Ross Rowland incorporated American Coal Enterprises to explore the possibilities of giving the railroads a viable "alternative fuel" locomotive in the wake of the 1970s oil crisis. His research team began with the N&W steam turbine and updated and improved it using modern computer technology. Calculations showed, however, that a new concept in a balanced reciprocating drive would be more efficient and economical. To gather a base of computer data for the "ACE 3000," in January 1985 C&O 4-8-4 614 was put to work on a series of tests on coal trains between Huntington and Hinton, West Virginia, on Chessie System's former-C&O main line. In temperatures dropping to 20-below-zero, the 614 never missed a trip. Here on January 24, 1985, she storms into Handley, West Virginia, with 120 westbound empty coal cars at 50 MPH. The computer data proved that a 1948 steam locomotive really does pound the daylights out of the track and cannot match the performance of a modern diesel-electric. It is much more spectacular to watch, however.

In 1996 the 614 ran a series of fall colors excursions on New Jersey Transit's former-Erie main line between Hoboken, New Jersey and Port Jervis, New York. In October 1996 the 614 is being photographed from a helicopter as it crosses Moodna Viaduct at Washingtonville, New York. *(Mike Del Vecchio)*

track, which proved with modern computer-documented accuracy that a 1948 4-8-4 will still pound the living daylights out of the track at 45 MPH!

The 614 tests produced more spectacular photography than solid scientific data, but the mere fact that they were performed got the Chessie System some much-needed public support in the economically hard-hit coal region. If the energy crisis had continued two more years the ACE 3000 might

well have been built, but the price of oil dropped and so did the ACE 3000 program.

In October 1996 the 614 began a new series of annual excursions for commuter train/bus operator New Jersey Transit over the former Erie Railroad main line between Hoboken, New Jersey, and Port Jervis, New York. With a train of modern commuter cars, the big 4-8-4 was given track speed and did some 80-MPH running through the spectacular

autumn foliage. There is still a lot of life left in Lima's last 4-8-4.

The Santa Fe "Super Northerns"

The Santa Fe got its first 4-8-4, 3751, in 1927 and soon went on to acquire a fleet of 14 more identical 73-inch drivered machines. In the spring of 1938 Baldwin delivered the first massive 3765 Class 4-8-4s with one-piece cast engine beds, roller bearings, 80-inch drivers and 300-psi boiler pressure. These were the first "Super Northerns" to combine all of those modern elements, and they produced 5450 indicated horsepower at 65 MPH. In 1943 and 1944, the Santa Fe bought its last new 4-8-4s that were essentially duplicates of the 3765s, but because of wartime restrictions on lightweight materials, the 2900–2929 were the heaviest 4-8-4s

ever built, weighing in at 510,700 pounds (compared to 423,000 for the original 3751, 499,600 for a 3765, and 476,050 for a CB&Q O5b).

In late 1938 the Santa Fe began a program of rebuilding its old 3751-Class Northerns with 80-inch drivers, roller bearings and new cast engine beds. The original 3751 itself got the treatment in August 1940, increasing her original 2,080 drawbar horsepower to 3,500 at 60 MPH. The rebuilt 3751s were assigned to the longest run on the railroad, the *Grand Canyon Limited* between Los Angeles and Wellington, Kansas—1,534 miles each way!

The rebuilt pioneer 3751 was working out of Los Angeles, Bakersfield, and San Diego in the early 1950s as diesels began to displace Santa Fe steam in the West, and by early 1954 she was dead. Many big Santa Fe steam locomotives were

The Santa Fe's first "super Northerns" were the 3765 class, ordered from Baldwin in 1937 with 80-inch drivers and 300-psi boiler pressure. The 3775 is shown heading up the eastbound *Chief* on Cajon Pass out of San Bernardino, California, in the 1940s. *(Santa Fe, Railfan & Railroad collection)*

(Above) The 3751 was the first 4-8-4 built by Baldwin and the first for the Santa Fe. As shown in this May 1927 builder's photo, the 3751 had 73-inch drivers and 210-psi boiler pressure. In August 1941 the 3751 emerged from rebuilding with 80-inch drivers and a 230-psi boiler, taking on the appearance it has to this day. *(Baldwin Locomotive Works)*

(Above) On June 14, 1999, the 3751 descended the famous Tehachapi Loop on its journey to participate in Railfair '99 at the California State Railroad Museum in Sacramento.

(Right) On December 27, 1991, the 3751 climbed Cajon Pass for the first time since being retired in the 1950s. It was on a four-day run from Los Angeles to Bakersfield and back.

donated to parks and museums from Chicago to California, and the 3751 wound up across from the handsome passenger station in San Bernardino, California.

In 1986 the San Bernardino Railroad Historical Society began a restoration project on the 3751 that would not be completed until December 1991. But it was worth the effort, for two days after Christmas 1991 the 3751 stormed out of Los Angeles and assaulted Cajon Pass again with a passenger train bound for Barstow and Bakersfield. Not bad for the oldest 4-8-4 in existence.

The Dazzling "Daylight"

While the Southern Pacific got its first "General Service" 4-8-4s (4400–4409) from Baldwin in 1930,

(Below) Southern Pacific GS4 4-8-4 4452 was still wearing its full *Daylight* streamlining in 1950 as it exited a tunnel near Pinole, California, along San Pablo Bay, en route from San Francisco to San Jose. SP introduced the colorful styling in 1936 for its fast new *Daylight* trains between Los Angeles and San Francisco and applied it to five different classes of Lima-built 4-8-4s. *(R. L. Borcherding, Railfan & Railroad collection)*

(Above) De-skirted "Black Daylight" 4464 is at Portland, Oregon, on September 6, 1948. *(D. H. Roberts)*

the six new GS2's (4410–4415) outshopped by Lima in 1936 were to power the SP's newest passenger train, the *Daylight* streamliner between Los Angeles and San Francisco. The engines wore a streamlined "skyline casing" over the top of the boiler, skirts on the running boards and a cone-shaped nose on the front—and all of that was painted in a blaze of orange, red, silver, and black.

Under all that make-up, however, was still the 73-inch-drivered 4-8-4 of 1930. The 14 GS3 engines (4416–4429) that came out of Lima in 1937 had the same colorful styling, but underneath there was a much more potent passenger engine. The drivers had been upped to 80 inches in diameter and the boiler pressure boosted from 250 to 280 psi. These new "Daylights"—as the locomotives themselves came to be known—could easily manage the 80-MPH schedule with the streamliners and still deal effectively with the older heavyweight trains.

In 1941 SP turned again to Lima for 28 new GS4's (4430–4457), nearly identical to the GS3's but having 300-psi boiler pressure and a very distinctive "face" created by putting two headlights on the conical nose. The top headlight was actually an oscillating safety light produced by the Mars Company that rotated in a horizontal figure-8 pattern to warn motorists at crossings of the oncoming train. In spite of their otherwise completely modern design, the SP 4-8-4s up to this point were inexplicably missing the one thing that would have made them state-of-the-art designs: roller bearings (though two were equipped with rollers as a test). Wartime restrictions against passenger engines caused the SP to go back to general service 73-inch drivers for its last new 4-8-4s, ten GS6's (4460–4469) in 1943.

Only two SP 4-8-4s survived, GS6 4460 in the National Museum of Transport in St. Louis and GS4 4449 in Oaks Park in Portland, Oregon. In Novem-

Restored to her dazzling *Daylight* livery for the first time after operating in *American Freedom Train* colors, Southern Pacific GS4 4449 spent April 25, 1981, at Portland Union Station before departing the next day for the grand opening of the California State Railroad Museum.

(Above) Southern Pacific 4449 was overhauled in 1974 to pull the *American Freedom Train*. In June 1975 it rolls along the Chicago & North Western at Waukegan, Illinois, en route to Green Bay, Wisconsin.

(Right) The 4449's speedometer is pegged at 66 MPH as it works the *Louisiana World's Fair Daylight* out of Klamath Falls, Oregon, on May 6, 1984.

(Far right) Engineer Doyle McCormack adjusts the reverse gear with the throttle wide open in April 1986 during the filming of the movie *Tough Guys* on the Eagle Mountain Railroad.

ber 1974 the 4449 was pulled out to power the *American Freedom Train* on its two-year 35,000-mile coast-to-coast trek for the 1976 Bicentennial celebration. She was overhauled by a crew headed up by Doyle McCormack, a young locomotive engineer off the Nickel Plate who had learned the steam trade by working on NKP Berkshire 759 in 1968. The 4449 toured the country wearing the *Freedom Train's* red, white, and blue livery, before being returned to Portland.

It was the gala opening of the new California State Railroad Museum in Sacramento in 1981 that brought the 4449 out on the road again—only this time she was in full *Daylight* livery in gleaming DuPont Imron paint. Even fresh from Lima, no Daylight locomotive had ever been so dazzling. The overwhelming public attention given the 4449 impressed even the hard-nosed and skeptical SP management, and over the next two decades the 4449 was permitted to venture out on special occasions, often accompanied by a complete matching *Daylight* streamlined train.

A Touch of Gray

The only mainline steam locomotive in America today that has been on its original owner's active roster since it was built is Union Pacific's 4-8-4 No. 844. She was also the last steam locomotive built for the UP, rolling out of Alco's Schenectady Works in December 1944.

The UP had worked closely with Alco to design

its first 4-8-4s in 1937, and the 20 oil-burning Class FEF-1 engines 800–819 were considered excellent machines with 77-inch drivers, 300-psi boiler pressure and roller bearings. But these "Little 800s" paled by comparison to the second batch, FEF-2s 820–834, turned out by Alco in 1939. The new engines had improved boilers and 80-inch drivers, and they were designed for continuous maximum horsepower output at 90 MPH—while the engineering calculations were based on sustained operation at 110 MPH! So successful were the new "Big 800s" that ten more (835–844) were built during World War II. The wartime FEF-3 engines differed from the FEF-2's only in minor details, such as the double-pipe smokestack. With 80-inch drivers and 300-psi boiler pressure, the UP Big 800s joined the Santa Fe 2900s and Southern Pacific GS4

In the late afternoon of May 11, 1968, Union Pacific 4-8-4 8444 rounds a curve near Rock River, Wyoming, on an excursion from Denver to Rawlins, sponsored by the Rocky Mountain Railroad Club. It had been built by Alco in December 1944 and was the UP's last new steam locomotive. As other steam was retired, the 8444 was kept active as a snow-melter and was tapped for excursion service in 1960. As a result, it is to this day the only operating North American steam locomotive that has never been retired from the active roster of its original owner.

Daylights as the only true Western "Super Northerns" in both size and performance.

After the war, the UP decided to "dress up" its passenger engines with an attractive two-tone gray paint scheme. As diesels displaced steam from passenger service in the early 1950s, the gray paint was replaced by conventional black as the 800s then proved to be excellent fast freight haulers, in spite of their 80-inch drivers.

The 800s were all retired by 1958—except the 844, which was equipped with snow-melting pipes for thawing track switches in the Council Bluffs, Iowa, yard. With her boiler still under current certification, the 844 was tapped for a railfan excursion in 1960. The UP kept the 844 in serviceable condition after that for public relations work. With the arrival of GP30 diesels in 1962 numbered in the 800 series, the 844 was renumbered 8444 and began creating a legend all her own.

Maintained by the regular roundhouse forces in Cheyenne, Wyoming, the 8444 seldom operated more than a half-dozen times a year until the early 1980s, when operating manager Steve Lee took over the steam program and built up a qualified staff of Union Pacific railroaders to maintain the 8444 with a formal budget approved by corporate management.

In 1987 Steve Lee made good on his often-voiced desire to return the engine to her 1940s pas-

In an effort to improve the image of its passenger steam locomotives as the diesel "streamliner" rage was sweeping the country, in 1946 Union Pacific introduced its "Greyhound" livery, which was applied to engines ranging from small 4-6-2s to huge 4-6-6-4s but was best known on the 4-8-4s. In 1987 the 8444 emerged from the Cheyenne shop in gray and pin-stripes rendered in gleaming Imron paint and reflectorized stripes. Her Greyhound debut was on a run from Denver to Laramie on October 3, 1987. In the low, late afternoon sun of that day, the 8444 is in the midst of a series of superb photo runbys at Hermosa, Wyoming, near the crest of Sherman Hill.

senger gray livery. The Grateful Dead had a hit record entitled "A Touch of Gray" on the radio as the engine headed out of Denver one October morning in 1987. The chorus included the words, "I will get by; I will survive." For UP's newest grey-hound, they were fitting, indeed.

In 1989, UP GP30 diesel 844 was retired to a museum, and Union Pacific's last steam locomo-tive got her rightful number back. She had worn her original number 18 years before getting the extra "4"—and had steamed through the diesel's entire working career of 27 years to get her original number restored! The 844 enters the new millen-nium as the only American steam locomotive in mainline service that was never retired by her orig-inal owner.

"Clinchfield 676" steams the night away in Huntington, West Virginia, on November 18, 1992. This 4-6-6-4 is actually Union Pacific 3985, cosmetically altered to represent a Clinchfield Challenger to help CSX celebrate the 50th Anniversary run of the Clinchfield's *Santa Claus Special* from Elkhorn City, Kentucky, to Johnson City, Tennessee.

5
Last of the
Giants

In an effort to make a large but flexible locomotive, in 1903 the American Locomotive Company built the first North American "Mallet articulated," which placed a hinge in the frame and provided two sets of cylinders and drivers (see page 46). The Mallet design was intended for a compound locomotive where hot steam from the boiler was fed at full pressure to the rear cylinders and then exhausted into the much larger front cylinders to be used again, producing a very powerful and efficient locomotive, although most were rather ponderous and slow.

The articulated design could ride well at higher speeds, however, and in 1924 Alco built the first "simple" articulated 2-8-8-2s for the C&O, with all four cylinders receiving high pressure steam directly from the boiler. In 1928 this concept was carried one step further by enlarging the firebox

and adding a four-wheel trailing truck to create huge 2-8-8-4s for the Northern Pacific, which named the type the "Yellowstone." Over the years, many fine 2-8-8-4s were designed and built, with most featuring 63- or 64-inch driving wheels capable of speeds around 60 MPH. Among the last of the Yellowstones to see service were the 18 impressive 350-ton Baldwins built for the Duluth, Missabe & Iron Range in 1941–43 and the 30 stylish Baltimore & Ohio EM1 engines of 1944.

Cab-Forwards

Perhaps the most unusual simple articulateds to run in America were the Southern Pacific's "backward Yellowstones." After earlier success with smaller articulateds, in 1928 the SP had Baldwin "turn around" a 2-8-8-4 to put the cab and firebox toward the front and couple the tender to the

Otto Jabelmann, Union Pacific's Vice President-Research & Mechanical Standards, poses with his pride and joy "Big Boy," the world's largest steam locomotive, as it was on public display in Omaha in September 1941. UP's 25 leviathan 4-8-8-4s were built in 1941 and 1944. Jabelmann designed the locomotive that has become a symbol of the American steam locomotive at its pinnacle.

(Left) The same low-grade coal that required a large firebox which prompted the Northern Pacific to create the first 4-8-4 with Alco in 1926 was also the reason they enlarged a 2-8-8-2 simple articulated into the first 2-8-8-4 in 1928. The result was what at that time was the world's largest steam locomotive. The wheel arrangement was named "Yellowstone" in honor of the National Park served by the NP. Alco built only the first locomotive, 5000, while Baldwin built the other eleven that made up the NP fleet. Yellowstone 5003 was pushing a heavy freight on an early morning in 1948, with the engineer taking train orders at the Bozeman, Montana, station. *(Frank McKinlay, Railfan & Railroad collection)*

The last Yellowstones were 30 compact and elegant Class EM1's turned out by Baldwin in 1944 and 1945 for the Baltimore & Ohio. With roller bearings and 64-inch drivers, they were used initially as fast freight engines. By December 1957, however, they had been bumped from the manifests by diesels and were working the coal trains out of Wheeling, West Virginia. Here the 651 is storming through Boydsville, Ohio, with a "humper" coal train from Benwood, West Virginia, upgrade out of the Ohio River valley to Holloway, Ohio. *(J. J. Young Jr.)*

During World War II, the Duluth, Missabe & Iron Range needed more-powerful locomotives to handle its iron-ore trains and bought eight 2-8-8-4s from Baldwin in 1941. Ten more were delivered in 1943, and they were the heaviest Yellowstones ever built. On a spring day in 1959, the 221 was bringing a loaded ore train into Proctor, Minnesota. Three of these magnificent engines have been preserved, and one is likely to return to service in the not-too-distant future. *(Russ Porter)*

(Above) The use of oil for fuel permitted the Southern Pacific to experiment with "turning around" Mallet articulateds so that the cab could run ahead of the smokestack through tunnels. This "Cab-Forward" idea was perfected by Baldwin in 1928 with ten 4-8-8-2 simple articulateds. By 1944 the SP would roster 195 of these unique machines. The 4164 is shown climbing into the Sierra Nevada east of Sacramento with a freight in the 1940s. *(Southern Pacific, Railfan & Railroad collection)*

(Right) Often three or four Cab-Forwards would be used to hoist a heavy freight up to Donner Summit on the main line between Sacramento, California, and Reno/Sparks, Nevada. Here a Cab-Forward is serving as a mid-train helper on Donner. The large flat deck is on the articulated portion of the frame that can swing from side to side as the drive wheels follow the curves. *(Southern Pacific, Railfan & Railroad collection)*

smokebox end. These "Cab-Forwards" (or "Cab-Aheads" as SP crews called them) carried the crew far ahead of the smokestack, which was a big advantage in working through tunnels. Fuel oil and boiler water were piped forward from the tender, and the cylinders drove the locomotive "in reverse," which was no problem. The only important change in creating a Cab-Forward from a Yellowstone was in replacing the radial trailing truck under the firebox with a center-pivot lead truck specifically designed to guide the locomotive through curves.

Baldwin built 195 of the fast and powerful SP Cab-Forwards between 1928 and 1944 (SP also bought a dozen conventional coal-fired 2-8-8-4s from Lima in 1939). Although intended primarily

for freight service, the Cab-Forwards were used extensively on passenger trains in the Sierra Nevada and Cascade Mountains and over the hills into Los Angeles.

Three Cylinders

In 1926 Union Pacific was looking for a big locomotive that could run faster than its ponderous compound 2-8-8-0s and turned to the three-cylinder 4-12-2. With 67-inch drivers, these long-legged monsters could deliver the power and still run at 60 MPH on the fairly straight prairie main lines. The third cylinder was placed in the saddle beneath the smokebox between the outer two cylinders and was connected to a crank on the second driving axle. The valve timing on the center cylinder was

Southern Pacific had a dozen conventional 2-8-8-4s built by Lima in 1939 that were essentially "backward Cab-Forwards" that burned coal. The 3811 is working westward out of Tucumcari, New Mexico, on June 5, 1940. These engines had real trailing trucks under the firebox, while the Cab-Forwards had a true lead truck with a different type of centering suspension. *(Richard Kindig)*

119

actuated by a "Gresley" valve gear that worked off the motion of the two outside valve stems. Because of the need for the center driving rod to clear the front driving axle, the center cylinder was elevated about 12 degrees above center, and when running this gave the three-cylinder locomotives an off-beat "1—2-3—4—5-6" exhaust sound instead of the even "1—2—3—4" of a conventional two-cylinder engine—or as photographer Don Ball once described the sound, "a washing-machine, a sewing-machine."

Modern three-cylinder locomotives became popular in the 1920s, with many built in the U.S., such as 4-8-2s for the Delaware, Lackawanna & Western and 4-10-2s for the Southern Pacific and Union Pacific. The mechanical complexity and difficulty in servicing the center cylinder and rod soon rendered three-cylinder locomotives in disfavor on most owning roads. Nonetheless, SP's 4-10-2s and UP's 4-12-2s had long and productive lives.

Ironically, the last three-cylinder locomotive to

operate on a main line in the U.S. was a London & North Eastern 4-6-2 designed by Sir Nigel Gresley, who had invented the valve gear that bears his name. The British *Flying Scotsman* toured the U.S. from coast to coast in 1969–70, bringing its distinctive "Gresley beat" exhaust to a continent that had not heard it in well over a decade.

The Challengers

Although its 90 4-12-2s were fine on straight and flat prairie railroad, the Union Pacific needed a locomotive that could develop that power and speed in the mountains. The railroad's General Mechanical Engineer Arthur H. Fetters envisioned a simple articulated that would use slightly higher drivers and lightweight rods to deliver the 4-12-2's power at greater speeds. Working closely with Alco, Fetters' team designed the first 4-6-6-4; its 69-inch drivers and other improvements would give it speed well over 70 MPH.

They were named "Challengers" after one of UP's passenger trains, and the name was very

appropriate because the 4-6-6-4s immediately proved themselves to be excellent dual-service locomotives capable of passenger train speeds. By 1937 the UP was operating 40 of the "Fetters" Challengers, but with the onset of World War II more motive power was needed. In 1942 Mr. Fetters' successor, Otto Jabelmann, created a much improved 4-6-6-4 with one-piece cast steel engine beds, roller bearings, and 280-psi boilers. Over the next two years, 65 of the Jabelmann "Super Challengers" were built, and the "War Babies" proved to be the

UP's most useful and versatile steam locomotives. Within their working lives both the Fetters and Jabelmann Challengers were fueled on both coal and oil, and worked right to the end of UP steam in the autumn of 1958.

One of the wartime Challengers was the 3985, built in July 1943. The coal-burning 3985 made her last revenue run in August 1957 and was held in Cheyenne for possible display. Within a few years, the 3985 and sister 3977 (now at North Platte, Nebraska) had become the last two 4-6-6-4s in

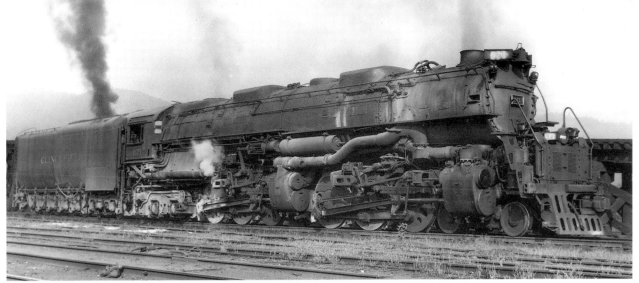

existence. In January 1975 the 3985 was placed on display outside the Cheyenne depot.

It was one of the shortest displays in history, for on September 24, 1979, she was returned to the Cheyenne roundhouse to begin restoration by a group of volunteer UP railroaders. On March 25, 1981, she rolled out under steam and joined the long-lived 4-8-4 8444 as part of the UP's active steam program. The 3985 was the largest steam locomotive to be restored to service anywhere in the twentieth century.

Because her coal fire produced hot cinders that

(Right) The engineer on Union Pacific 4-6-6-4 3985 was preparing to back up for a photo runby while climbing east on Sherman Hill on June 18, 1988.

(Below) Pausing before the Sherman Hill photo runby on June 18, 1988, the 3985's sheer majesty is evident when you get close to it from almost any angle, and when it runs, you can understand why the Union Pacific invested in 105 of the versatile and speedy Challengers.

The 3985 was just another Challenger when this undated photo was taken at the crest of Archer Hill east of Cheyenne. The 3985 was in revenue freight service in the Cheyenne–North Platte pool after undergoing a Class 3 overhaul in April 1956. Records show her last revenue move was in August 1957, but the 3985 was not stricken from the active roster until 1959. It spent the next 16 years stored in the Cheyenne roundhouse as part of the UP's historic collection.

tended to set lineside grass fires, in 1990 she was converted to burn fuel oil, which solved that problem and made possible ventures all over the rapidly expanding UP system. In her modern-day rambles, the 3985 has often demonstrated why the UP bought 105 Challengers. Capable of awesome power and impressive acceleration, the 3985 rides like a Pullman sleeping car at 65 MPH.

Simple articulateds make very interesting sounds when they run. A compound articulated sounds like an ordinary two-cylinder locomotive, since the steam exhausted through the stack is from only the front set of low pressure cylinders. On a simple articulated like the 3985, however, all four cylinders exhaust through the stack. And since the front and rear engines are not mechanically linked together, they operate independently of one another and sound like two locomotives double-headed. Sometimes the two engines will be "in step," and the 3985 will sound like a 4-8-4, but then one of the engines will creep out of synchronization and a double-beat exhaust will result, giving eight beats per revolution of the drivers instead of four. Listening to the engines work in and out of "step" makes the 3985 one of America's most fascinating locomotives to ride behind or hear from lineside.

Roanoke's "Big Three"

While Alco, Baldwin, and Lima were exploring the limits of steam locomotive design, deep in the mountains of the Virginias the Norfolk & Western was rather single-mindedly moving coal out of the hollows. By the early 1920s it had settled on the USRA compound 2-8-8-2 as its primary road engine with some USRA Heavy 4-8-2s for passenger service. Around 1930 the N&W stopped buying from the commercial builders and began concentrating on building new locomotives in its own Roanoke Shops.

The evening sun was low as the 3985—heading an excursion train—swept downhill around the great curve at Buford, Wyoming, on the east slope of Sherman Hill west of Cheyenne on June 18, 1988. The oil smoke traced the S-curve in the warm but dead still air.

Reviving a Clinchfield Challenger

Although the first Challengers were designed by and for the Union Pacific, other railroads adopted the obviously successful wheel arrangement. Challengers were built by Alco for the Northern Pacific; Delaware & Hudson; Western Pacific; Spokane, Portland & Seattle; and the Clinchfield Railroad, while Baldwin Locomotive Works turned out similar machines for the Denver & Rio Grande Western and Western Maryland. Today, only two Challengers survive, both of which belonged to UP.

On the night of June 17, 1988, however, a Clinchfield Challenger mysteriously appeared. During World War II, six 4-6-6-4s were added by Alco to the UP order that included the 3985, and those six were delivered to the Denver & Rio Grande Western. Those, identical to the 3985 and its sisters, had fireboxes configured to burn low-grade Wyoming coal, which the Rio Grande did not use. As a result, the D&RGW was not entirely happy with their performance. Preferring its own Baldwin-built 4-6-6-4s, the Rio Grande immediately after the war sold the six Alcos to the Clinchfield, which also had a fleet of its own smaller Challengers. (The Clinchfield was a 277-mile Appalachian coal-hauler running from Elkhorn City, Kentucky, south to Spartanburg, North Carolina.)

In 1988 a group of Appalachian railfans led by Steve Patterson and Ron Flanary persuaded the UP to let them reletter the 3985 as "Clinchfield 675" for a night photography session. The Clinchfield's ex-D&RGW challengers had been 670-675, and the latter had been a boyhood favorite of Patterson. A new front number board was put on over the UP's shield, a visor was added to the headlight, and large rolls of paper carrying the CLINCHFIELD lettering were applied to the left side of the tender and cab. For two hours the calendar was repealed on the night of June 17, 1988, and Clinchfield 4-6-6-4 675 was alive under steam, albeit in Cheyenne, Wyoming. The next day the 3985 stormed Sherman Hill with no evidence of her transformation of the night before.

But it would get better. One of the men who had been responsible for preserving the steam program under the umbrella of the Union Pacific parent corporation was Jerry Davis, who had just moved to a new position as president of CSX Corporation, which now owned the old Clinchfield. For 49 years the Clinchfield had been operating annual "Santa Claus Specials" with the jolly old elf dispensing gifts and candy to kids in the Appalachian communities along the railroad. CSX fully supported continuing the community effort, and the aforementioned Patterson and Flanary planted the idea with Jerry Davis that the return of a Clinchfield 4-6-6-4 would be a spectacular way to celebrate the 50th Anniversary Santa Train. Mr. Davis still had considerable influence with his friends on the Union Pacific and knew well the capabilities and limitations of the 3985.

And so it was that on November 19, 1992, "Clinchfield 676" steamed out of Huntington, West Virginia, en route to Clinchfield Country, where Challengers had been absent for decades. The world's largest operating steam locomotive looked right at home where her six 1943 shop-mates had spent most of their working lives. It was living proof that almost anything is possible with the steam locomotives that have been preserved.

"That's Clinchfield train 97, the *Florida Perishable*, ready to leave Erwin," is how Appalachian Ron Flanary described this scene as he stood there in Huntington, West Virginia, on November 18, 1992, with UP 4-6-6-4 3985 disguised as "Clinchfield 676." The next day the engine would head up Clinchfield's *Santa Claus Special*.

Quite satisfied with the tremendous power of the USRA 2-8-8-2s in low-speed coal service, in 1936 the N&W applied the modern concepts of cast engine beds and roller bearings to the basic USRA compound, increasing its drivers by one inch to 58 inches and upping its 270-psi boiler to 300 psi. Additionally, the new Y6-class 2-8-8-2s had the most modern of lubrication systems to reduce maintenance between runs.

That same year, 1936, the N&W borrowed a wheel arrangement pioneered by the Seaboard Air Line and created a massive 2-6-6-4 simple articulated with 70-inch drivers for fast freight service. Unlike the UP 4-6-6-4, with its firebox cramped above the rear drivers, the N&W 2-6-6-4 had its huge firebox completely behind the drivers. This tremendous furnace combined with a big combustion chamber produced a boiler of awesome capacity. The roller-bearing-equipped running gear gave the locomotive the capability of delivering that power at speeds up to 70 MPH The 2-6-6-4 wheel arrangement was never given a name (and was duplicated only on the SAL and the P&WV), and on the N&W it was simply known as the "Class A." Forty-four Class A's were built between 1936 and 1950. What the compound Y6's could muscle over the mountains, the A's could sprint across the Virginia hills to Tidewater or the Ohio cornfields to Columbus. Between the A's and Y6's, the N&W had a fleet of modern articulateds perfectly suited to its needs.

By 1941 the diesel had proven itself a capable competitor, but the N&W, which owed its prosper-

Norfolk & Western resorted to pure muscle to get its heavy coal trains over the 1.2 percent Blue Ridge grade east of Roanoke, Virginia. A pair of modern Y6 2-8-8-2's head a coal train on the hill near Blue Ridge summit on September 1, 1956. *(Gordon S. Crowell)*

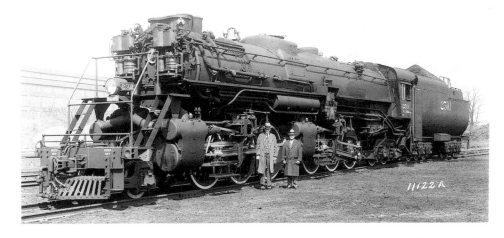

The 2-6-6-4 was not a common wheel arrangement, being built only for the Pittsburgh & West Virginia (a mountain-winding carrier) and Seaboard Air Line (a largely rolling-terrain railroad). Seaboard 2501 posed for its builder's photo at Baldwin in 1935. All ten of the SAL 2-6-6-4s were sold to the B&O in 1947. *(Baldwin Locomotive Works)*

There's nothing like a broadside view to show what an articulated steam locomotive is all about! Norfolk & Western Class A 2-6-6-4s featured fireboxes of awesome volume and boilers of tremendous capacity. The Class A was an unusually successful design in that they were used in precisely the service for which they had been designed. That service was never envisioned as being on excursion passenger trains, but on November 7, 1987, N&W 1218 was crossing the old Atlantic Coast Line in Valdosta, Georgia, as it turned on the Southern Railway wye to prepare for its return to Jacksonville on a North Florida Chapter-NRHS excursion trip.

Norfolk & Western Class J 611 was eastbound for Roanoke as it crossed the Roanoke River west of Salem, Virginia, on November 1, 1982, as a coal train headed west on the opposite track of the N&W main line.

ity to coal, was not about to abandon steam without a fight. The diesel's biggest advantage was its ability to operate great distances with no servicing or maintenance (often 500 to 1,000 miles), while the best steam locomotives required a couple of hours on the service tracks every 300 or 400 miles. The N&W set about to extend the service "range" of its locomotives through the use of roller bearings and advanced lubrication systems. These were designed into the 2-6-6-4s and 2-8-8-2s as

well as a fleet of new passenger locomotives, the Class J 4-8-4s, introduced in 1941.

The J was no ordinary 4-8-4. Beneath the tastefully streamlined black boiler with a Tuscan red band was one of the most advanced steam locomotives ever conceived. Its boiler had great steaming capacity, and its 70-inch drivers could deliver the power with snappy acceleration in the 40-MPH range that much of the mountainous and curving main line required. But by using lightweight, roller-

bearing-equipped rods and an advanced theory of counterbalancing that included the use of the pilot and trailer trucks to enhance stability, the J was able to get 100-MPH speeds out of its relatively low drivers. It would be difficult to refute the N&W's proud claim that the J was the "finest steam passenger locomotive ever built." While the Santa Fe might have argued that point with its huge 100-MPH 80-inch-drivered 4-8-4s, there is no doubt that the J was the perfect locomotive for the N&W.

With the A, J, and Y6, by 1948 the N&W had its own "Big Three" handling over 90 percent of its total traffic. As the commercial builders were rolling out their very last steam locomotives in 1949 and turning their erecting halls over to diesel production, Roanoke was continuing to build new steam locomotives. The last of the 44 Class A 2-6-6-4s was outshopped in 1950, as was the 14th and last Class J 4-8-4. The final production version of the 2-8-8-2, the famous Y6b class of 1948, was the most advanced compound articulated ever built, and Roanoke kept building them into 1952!

It is one of the ironies of steam history, however, that Roanoke's last steam locomotive—and the last new steam locomotive built in America for domestic use—was not an A or J or Y6b. In December 1953 Roanoke outshopped the 244, an 0-8-0 switch engine copied from a 1918 USRA design borrowed from the C&O. There was a change in management shortly thereafter, and diesels displaced most N&W steam by 1959. The fires went out completely in 1960.

Today, there is only one example of each of Roanoke's "Big Three" in existence—but two of them have been under steam! Although the older 1923-built Y3 2-8-8-2 2050 is preserved at the Illinois Railway Museum near Chicago, the only modern Y6 remaining is the 1942 Y6a 2156 at the National Museum of Transport in St. Louis, where

it has been beautifully restored as a non-operating display. Its huge size and top speed of 30 MPH would not make the 2156 a particularly useful excursion locomotive, however.

Class J 611 had been donated to the Roanoke Transportation Museum after night photographer O. Winston Link prodded N&W's then-new president Stuart Saunders to save the 4-8-4. The Class A 1218 avoided the scrappers by a more circuitous route and ended up back in Roanoke in 1967. Both the 611 and 1218 were in the Roanoke Transportation Museum when Robert B. Claytor became

(Above) You can't live much closer to the track than these folks in Boyertown on Southern Railway's branch from Manassas to Front Royal, Virginia. In spite of her size and power, the articulation permits N&W 2-6-6-4 1218 to easily negotiate the curves of this hill-country line with an excursion on May 15, 1988.

(Left) Robert B. Claytor was Chairman and CEO of Norfolk Southern as he took the throttle of N&W 4-8-4 611 from Iaeger to Bluefield, West Virginia, on October 30, 1982. The entire NS steam program was running under his direct authority as "The Boss."

president and CEO of the N&W in October 1981, and he immediately ordered the 611 to the Birmingham Steam Shop to become part of the Southern Railway steam program inaugurated in 1966 by his older brother Graham. The Southern and N&W were merged in March 1982 into the Norfolk Southern Corporation, with Bob Claytor as its chairman and CEO. That same year Graham Claytor became president of Amtrak. Soon the 1218 was moved to Birmingham, and it emerged under steam in April 1987. Since then, both ranged far and wide over the Norfolk Southern system under the auspices of the corporate steam program.

Although the J may have been impressive running the old Wabash main line into Kansas City and the A an unbelievable sight rambling through people's front lawns on Southern's Front Royal branch, neither looked better than when running on the

(Above) Norfolk & Western streamlined 4-8-4 611 fills the main street of Orange, Virginia, with a flood of sound from its booming whistle. The excursion is bound for Charlottesville on the Southern Railway.

(Left) The rocky bluffs above the New River form an impressive backdrop for N&W 611 as it works westward with an excursion run at Pembroke, Virginia, in October 1982. The engine is about to plunge into a tunnel through that rock face to short-cut a sharp bend in the river on the N&W main between Roanoke and Bluefield.

135

The Allegheny

When they were both running between 1987 and 1994, it was good sport to compare Union Pacific 4-6-6-4 3985 and Norfolk & Western 2-6-6-4 1218 (the UP is bigger and faster, while the N&W was more powerful), but the most interesting comparison would have been between the N&W A and its arch-rival, the Chesapeake & Ohio 2-6-6-6 "Allegheny." In fact, for many years the 1218 sat in the Roanoke museum right beside one of the two surviving C&O Alleghenies, the 1604. Entire books have been written comparing the two, as they were used in nearly identical service on adjacent railroads at the same time.

Adding to this rivalry is the fact that Lima built the 2-6-6-6 in 1941 more to "outperform the N&W A" than to meet the C&O's true traffic needs. The consensus seems to be that "Lima's Finest" did, indeed, have the potential to outperform the A—and nearly any other steam locomotive ever built, for that matter—but it was never utilized by the C&O to its full potential. And the Allegheny achieved its size and power at the expense of having the heaviest axle-loading of any steam locomotive ever built, which severely limited it to operating only on the very best constructed main lines. The N&W A, however, worked to its last days doing precisely the job for which it had been so well designed.

With the C&O 1604 now at the B&O Museum in Baltimore and the 1601 inside the Henry Ford Museum in Dearborn, Michigan, the opportunity for a side-by-side competition is highly unlikely. But even "stuffed and mounted," a C&O 2-6-6-6 is an awesome encounter. While the N&W A has a clean and lanky look, the C&O engine packs a massive pile of machinery on its pilot deck and smokebox front, and there few sights in railroading as impressive as that six-wheel trailing truck beneath

It was not an awesome Class A 2-6-6-4 or sleek streamlined Class J 4-8-4 speedster that was the last steam locomotive built for a U.S. railroad, but rather a copy of a second-hand World War I switch engine. In December 1953, N&W's Roanoke Shop completed 0-8-0 No. 244, the sister of these two working the passenger station lead tracks in front of the N&W company office building in Roanoke in 1958.

home rails of N&W. The J's soft exhaust bespoke of her inner efficiency as she glided through the valleys of Virginia, and the A's distinctive "hoot" whistle in the mountains was the very voice of the steam era. The knowledgeable person could appreciate that the J was the world's most powerful 4-8-4 in terms of tractive effort and that the A may have the most powerful boiler in service since 1960, but the sights and sounds they created on Christiansburg Mountain could be appreciated by anyone.

Unfortunately, after Bob Claytor died in 1993, and his brother Graham passed away in 1994, the company gracefully closed out the steam program in December 1994. This wrapped up 28 years of Southern/Norfolk Southern steam kicked off by Graham in 1966.

(Above) Chesapeake & Ohio 2-6-6-6 "Allegheny" 1656 works a freight from Toledo to Columbus through Fostoria, Ohio, in July 1952. (J. J. Young Jr.)

(Left) The Virginian Railway bought eight duplicates of the C&O 2-6-6-6s in 1945. The 903, at Roanoke, clearly shows the impressive six-wheel trailing truck. The Alleghenies on both railroads had the highest axle-loadings of any steam locomotive. (J. J. Young Jr.)

(Above) The 6-4-4-6 "Big Engine" 6100, built in 1939, was the Pennsylvania Railroad's first duplex. It is shown at Englewood station in Chicago with the westbound *Broadway Limited*. *(Cal's Classics)*

the huge firebox. From that standpoint, the Allegheny would win any contest on looks alone.

The Departed Giants

While fine examples of almost every stage of steam locomotive development have been preserved, there is one important type missing: the duplex. A "duplex" is similar to a simple articulated in that it has four cylinders and two sets of drivers. But a duplex has no hinge, and all the cylinders and drivers are aligned on one rigid frame. The purpose of the duplex was to apply greater power to the dri-

vers at high speed by dividing up the "drive" into smaller and more lightweight rod assemblies. Instead of a 4-8-4 with two cylinders and necessarily heavy rods, a duplex 4-4-4-4 would have smaller cylinders and lighter rods, permitting higher speeds without the "pounding" of the rails that was characteristic of the steam locomotive.

The first duplexes were built in the mid-1930s by the B&O and Pennsylvania Railroad, but only the PRR continued the study and produced any number of working locomotives. In 1939 the PRR created its "Big Engine," 6-4-4-6 6100. Still dispatching its passenger trains with 1914-design K4s 4-6-2s, the PRR was seeking a fast and powerful new passenger engine. The 84-inch-drivered 6-4-4-6 developed a whopping 6,500 horsepower at 100 miles per hour—a performance that rather substantially exceeded service requirements.

To bring the power of the 6100 into a more useful package, the Pennsylvania went on to produce 52 4-4-4-4 duplexes—PRR Class T1—between 1942 and 1946 with 80-inch drivers and new rotary "poppet" valves instead of the conventional Walschaerts valve gear. Streamlined with distinctive shark-like noses, the T1's did, indeed, perform

(Right) The Pennsylvania Railroad was developing the duplex concept when diesels rendered the entire subject moot. After outshopping two experimental T1 4-4-4-4s in 1942, the PRR made a commitment to 50 more in 1945. With 80-inch drivers and rotary cam poppet valves, they were very fast—but quirky and costly to maintain. The 5536 is at Chicago in 1947. *(F. Smarz, Charles T. Felstead collection)*

spectacularly and displaced scores of K4s's. The T1's had their problems—they were very slippery and smoky—but it was only the arrival of the diesel that prevented their further development. Judging by the stories that have been told, the true world steam speed record was probably set on one night in the late 1940s when an engineer with a T1 was trying to make up time on the Fort Wayne Division and pushed his duplex over 130 MPH. The engines had a known tendency to develop violent high-speed wheel slips that damaged the poppet valves at track speeds over 120 MPH!

Probably the most spectacular of the PRR's duplexes, however, were the huge "Q2" 4-4-6-4s. After experimenting in 1942 with two "Q1" 4-6-4-4s with the rear cylinders behind the drivers—creating the appearance of a 77-inch-drivered 4-10-4—the PRR built 25 Q2s in 1945 with 69-inch drivers and each set of cylinders placed in front of its drivers. They produced nearly 8,000 horsepower and were quite possibly the most powerful boilers ever placed on a steam locomotive. Unfortunately, no

American duplexes of any configuration were saved when the diesels caused their premature demise in the mid-1950s. But if the diesel hadn't killed steam and it had been permitted to develop, the Q2 was probably as close to "tomorrow" as the steam locomotive ever got.

Big Boy

As almost any schoolboy knows, the Challenger was not the Union Pacific's biggest steam locomotive. That honor belongs to the "Big Boy" 4-8-8-4s of September 1941, the largest steam locomotives ever built. In just a little over a year, Otto Jabelmann's mechanical design department created a locomotive that could "pull 3,600 tons over the Wahsatch unassisted," where a Challenger was good for about 3,110 tons.

The 4-8-8-4 included all the most modern elements from a 300-psi boiler with a huge combustion chamber to cast engine beds and roller bearings. Riding on 68-inch drivers, the Big Boys attained speeds of 80 MPH, though most of their

There were five Union Pacific 4-8-8-4 Big Boys under steam in the engine terminal at Laramie, Wyoming, on August 20, 1957. In the warm evening air, the 4017 was simmering beneath the huge coaling tower with another Big Boy lined up behind it. As powerful gas turbines and new diesels took over more and more of the traffic, the Big Boys would prevail for only two more years before being silenced. The summer of 1959 would be the last season for steam on the Union Pacific over Sherman Hill, where the Big Boys wrote their own page in the history books as the world's largest steam locomotives. *(Jim Shaughnessy)*

Summer usually brought a boom in traffic to the Union Pacific, and on July 8, 1959, Big Boy 4019 was departing Cheyenne, bound for one last season on Sherman Hill. Until two days earlier, the Big Boys and Challengers had been in storage in the Cheyenne roundhouse. *(Larry McMurtry)*

heavy work was done between 30 and 50 MPH where they developed their greatest horsepower (over 6,000 drawbar horsepower at 35 MPH).

War was already brewing in Europe when the nearly-completed UP 4000 was on the erecting floor at Schenectady, and an Alco machinist chalked a "V" for Victory on the smokebox along with the words "Big Boy!" The name stuck. The first 20 Big Boys (4000–4019) were turned out between September 1941 and January 1942, and five more (4020–4024) came along in late 1944. The coal-

burning Big Boys were used almost exclusively as heavy freight locomotives, and it is interesting to note that the UP designed and purchased all 65 of the Jabelmann Super Challengers after the first 20 Big Boys had been built, finding the 4-6-6-4 a more versatile locomotive.

Although there were lower drivered locomotives that had more tractive effort and smaller locomotives that developed more boiler horsepower, there is no doubt that Otto Jabelmann's 386-ton Big Boys will be forever recognized as "the world's largest

steam locomotives." In addition to that, they performed better than their designers had expected and proved to be all-around "good" locomotives that served the UP very well.

Of the 25 Big Boys built, eight have survived, scattered as far and wide as California, Texas, and Pennsylvania. But since retired by the UP, none has operated under steam. In 1984, however, the 4012 made a 335-mile journey from Bellows Falls, Vermont, to the new home of Steamtown U.S.A. in Scranton, Pennsylvania, and the trouble-free move behind a diesel showed the 4012 to be a prime candidate for restoration, and it is one of the few Big Boys located in a museum that has a railroad substantial enough to run it on. In the mid-1990s, a movie production company began working on the 4018 at the Age of Steam Railroad Museum in Dallas, Texas.

Will the 4012 or 4018—or any other Big Boy—ever run again?

Absolutely.

Why?

Like Mount Everest, because it's there.

On Memorial Day 1999, UP Big Boy 4012 was posed for a night photo session at the Steamtown National Historic Site in Scranton, Pennsylvania. Of the eight Big Boys saved, this one may run again.

The history of the steam locomotive as described in this book is summed up in this one scene in the Henry Ford Museum in Dearborn, Michigan. On the left is a replica of the *DeWitt Clinton*, which on August 9, 1831, was the first locomotive to operate in New York State, and on the right is Chesapeake & Ohio 2-6-6-6 1601, one of the last of the giants.

Index